About the author

David Bonham-Carter is a life coach and writer on self-help topics who specializes in helping people struggling with assertiveness, self-esteem, anxiety and related difficulties. For many years David worked in the UK as a social worker helping people from a range of backgrounds to achieve positive changes in their lives through face-to-face work before setting up his own life coaching practice in Bristol. He has a Masters Degree in Social Work from the University of Kent (passed with distinction) and a Masters Degree in Philosophy from the University of Bristol. He has a particular interest in the use of cognitive behavioural therapy (CBT) techniques for helping people to develop self-esteem and assertiveness skills and he has written a number of guides to dealing with particular emotional and cognitive difficulties. More information about his life coaching service and his practical self-help guides is available at his website www.davidbonham-carter.com

David would like to thank Denise for her helpful comments on the first draft of this book.

Author's note

It is important to note that there are many ideas frequently cited in relation to assertiveness. I have sought to give credit to the original sources of ideas where known. My apologies to the originators of any ideas who have been inadvertently overlooked.

Contents

checklist to address anxiety – Facing up to your
fears of being assertive – Positive visualization –
How to get your point across – The DEAL method

Introduction

Assertiveness is about how you act in relationships and how effectively you communicate. Imagine what it would be like if you could express your wishes, feelings and thoughts in ways that improved your chances of getting what you want without infringing the rights of others. How would you feel if you could be truer to yourself, stand up for your rights and resist attempts by others to put you down or take you for granted? Assertiveness involves doing these things while at the same time listening to others and acting towards them with respect and honesty.

This book discusses some of the issues involved in behaving and communicating assertively. It explains ideas and methods that you can follow and practise to help you become more assertive. It examines:

- Specific techniques for developing assertive behaviour

- Specific techniques for changing your behaviour in situations where you have a tendency to act non-assertively by being either:
  - Too passive (not assertive enough) or
  - Directly aggressive (unduly forceful, through physically or verbally disrespecting the rights of others), or
  - Indirectly aggressive (disrupting situations in subtler ways or by influencing and controlling people with manipulation).

1

What is assertiveness?

If you are assertive then you:

- Stand up for your own and other people's rights in a reasonable and clear way in situations where it is appropriate to do so

- Express your views clearly and articulately without being aggressive

- Give other people a reasonable opportunity to express their opinions without letting them dominate a conversation

- Have the courage to express your own feelings and thoughts when it is appropriate, even about difficult issues, and to do so in a way which is respectful and honest.

The benefits of being assertive

There are many potential benefits to being assertive, including:

- Feeling more confident

- Being able to relax more

- Having greater awareness of your own needs and a greater ability to meet them

- Being able to create personal and professional goals instead of putting everyone else first or getting distracted by other priorities and different agendas

- Participating in honest, constructive relationships where you and others can develop understanding and respect and solve problems together.

Ways of behaving that are not assertive

1. Passive behaviour

Passive behaviour is a type of behaviour which is characteristic of people who seek to avoid conflict or criticism. If this is a form of behaviour which you often adopt then it is likely that whatever your own feelings you may allow others to make choices and decisions for you or to take advantage of your goodwill.

If you act passively then you are likely to do things such as:

- Go along with other people's decisions even if you don't agree with them because you don't want to have an argument

- Take on an excessive share of unpleasant or mundane tasks because you feel that it would be confrontational to say 'no' or you are worried about the consequences of saying 'no'

- Agree to do things you don't want to do, because you are overly concerned with trying to please people or don't want to upset them

- Fail to express or communicate your true feelings (particularly when these involve contradicting another person or criticizing them) because of anxieties about the effect on your relationship or worries that people may then have a negative opinion of you

- Fail to exercise your rights or remain unaware of them or believe that you should always be deferential or compliant towards others.

2. Aggressive behaviour

Aggressive behaviour is the opposite of passive behaviour: it involves seeking to have your own wishes met irrespective of the needs or wishes of others and without showing reasonable respect. Behaviour can be **directly aggressive** – for example, when someone speaks in a loud or intimidating manner, making demands – or it can be **indirectly aggressive** – for example, when someone covertly, deceitfully or in a manner that plays on other people's emotions, steers events towards what they themselves want in a self-centred way.

If you act with **direct aggression** then you may do any or all of the following things:

- Dominate conversations, interrupt other people and not give them the opportunity to speak

- Shout or use abusive language towards other people when they don't act in a way you agree with or they challenge what you are saying

- Find it difficult to acknowledge your faults or errors and act defensively when criticized reasonably

- Use intimidating body language or threats, or assault others when they do not do what you want or as a way of trying to coerce them or express your disapproval

- Show little regard for the rights of others and treat them without much respect.

Indirectly aggressive behaviour, on the other hand, involves behaviour which at first sight is not so obviously abusive or aggressive but which can be equally disruptive or controlling of others through less overt means. Acting with **indirect aggression** may involve doing things such as:

- Lying or painting distorted pictures of people or situations in order to convey a particular impression or achieve results you want

- Making out that you are a victim or have been hard done by in cases where this is not so, in order to achieve sympathy or to pressurize others into acting in certain ways

- Playing on other people's insecurities or potential feelings of guilt, anxiety, shame or fear in order to get them to do what you would like

- Committing to do things to achieve agreements with others even though you don't intend to carry through your commitments

- Playing innocent or misdescribing what you have agreed to previously, so as to cover up your own part in creating a problematic situation.

Problems arising from non-assertive behaviour

There may be some **short-term benefits** from behaving non-assertively, for example:

- If you behave passively you may avoid *immediate* confrontations

- If you behave with overt, direct aggression you may *sometimes* find that people don't argue with you (out of fear) and you get your way

- If you behave disruptively or manipulatively (i.e. with *indirect* aggression) you may sometimes get your way.

However, these benefits are often *transitory* or outweighed by more **significant or long-term drawbacks** arising from the way you have acted.

- You may frustrate or annoy people if you act passively or manipulatively, because you are not clearly or honestly expressing what you want

- You may allow yourself to take on too many commitments if you have passive tendencies, and then not be able to do everything you have promised

- You may anger or frighten people if you act aggressively

- You may be disregarded or marginalized if you act passively, because people learn that they can treat you like a doormat without significant repercussions

- You may be ignored or mistrusted if you act disruptively or manipulatively, because people may learn that you have a tendency to act in selfish or deceitful ways

- You may lose or not develop real lasting friendships through being over-passive, aggressive or manipulative, because important clear communication and honest respect are missing when you act in these ways.

For these reasons if you can learn to act more assertively and to change your non-assertive ways of behaving it can help you to improve:

- The quality of your relationships
- The effectiveness of your actions and
- The depth of respect in which you are held by others.

Building your assertiveness
The aim of this book is to give you ideas that can help you to become more assertive.

Section 1 details some proactive approaches to becoming more assertive:

Chapter 1 explores how to stand up for your rights, while respecting the rights and needs of others.

Chapter 2 takes you through some key aspects of communicating effectively.

Chapter 3 describes specific techniques for helping you to express yourself assertively and illustrates them through the use of case studies.

Section 2 examines particular types of non-assertive behaviour and explains what you can do to change your behaviour if you act in any of those particular non-assertive ways:

Chapter 4 is for people who have a tendency to act *passively* and allow their own needs and wishes to be submerged. The chapter provides different techniques that you can use to challenge your passivity appropriately and to become more assertive.

Chapter 5 explores how to modify and control your tendencies to *aggressive* behaviour if you are overtly aggressive in the way you act, and explains what you can do if your tendency is towards indirect aggression (disruptive or manipulative behaviour).

Chapter 6 describes how *low self-esteem* can be a factor contributing to your passive behaviour and how *excessively* *high* or *'pseudo' self-esteem* can be a factor in aggressive behaviour. The chapter gives ideas for countering the potential negative impact on your assertiveness if either of these self-esteem imbalances applies to you.

The **conclusion** shows you how you can bring together the lessons of the previous chapters and any particular techniques that are relevant to the situations that you face to create your own assertiveness plan.

Emotional responses and a reasoned approach to assertiveness

If you suffer from difficulties in being assertive then the likelihood is that that you have strong feelings such as *anxiety*, inhibiting you from expressing what you want and leading you to act passively, or *anger*, leading you to go the other way and be aggressive. When faced with strong, almost overwhelming feelings that paralyse you or seem to control your behaviour, it can be difficult to find a way to change. Training yourself to be assertive involves following practical exercises to help you deal with these difficult emotions.

This book builds in particular on the ideas of the psychologist Albert Ellis, the founder of a school of therapy known as 'Rational Emotive Behaviour Therapy'. Ellis argued that your *emotions* are often generated by the *thoughts* that you have, such as anxious thoughts about how events might turn out, or what people might think of you if you act in a certain way. Ellis showed that by a reasoned approach to analysing and addressing thought patterns that generate difficult emotions, you can help yourself to act in a way that is healthy, constructive and conducive to your personal development.

This book follows a similar reasoned approach to help you be more assertive, providing clear, structured exercises to help you change your behaviour and address thought patterns and emotions which may be making it difficult for you to be assertive.

How to use this book

The book is written as a guide to what assertiveness involves and how to become more assertive. Each chapter includes exercises and tips for you to follow and try out, with examples. The book is set out in a logical order that also allows you to focus on what is most important for you. If there is a particular chapter or chapters that you think may be relevant for you, then you can spend more time on that chapter or chapters, to glean the most from the ideas. For example, if you think that you have a tendency to behave passively, you may decide to focus in particular on chapter 3 (assertiveness techniques), chapter 4 (changing passive behaviour) and chapter 6 (self-esteem issues).

Where helpful, case studies are included. The people in the case studies are not real individuals but their dilemmas and efforts reflect concerns and approaches that are common.

Assessing your assertiveness

Very few (if any) people are assertive *all* of the time. There may well be some situations where you find it easier to be assertive or some people with whom you find it easier to communicate more effectively and assertively and vice versa. Later on in chapters 4 and 5, you will be asked to identify the kinds of situations where you might act passively or aggressively and you will be given ideas for how you can address problems in those particular situations. First, however, it may be useful for you to answer a few questions which will give you an idea of whether you have a general tendency to respond in one particular way.

 Read through the five questions below and write down an honest answer to each, describing how you would be most likely to react in the situation described. Appendix 2 sets out some possible ways in which people might react to each situation and how their responses might be classified in terms of assertiveness, using the four categories: passive, directly aggressive, indirectly aggressive and assertive. Compare your likely responses with those given in appendix 2, to help you decide whether you have a general tendency to act in a particular way. Alternatively, your answers may help you to see that in certain types of situation you act assertively, but in other situations you tend to act passively or aggressively.

1. At work a project comes up that you are very interested in working on. Your team leader asks everyone in the team if they would like to be involved. You and two others say 'yes' when asked. What do you then do, given that you want to be involved but so do others?

2. You and your partner are at a restaurant having a meal with friends. During the meal your partner keeps making dismissive remarks towards you. How do you react?

3. You receive an unsolicited telephone call from a caller offering a service to install solar glazing panels on your roof, which you have no interest in. How do you respond?

4. You are watching your favourite television programme when your flatmate comes in, takes the remote control, asks if you mind watching another programme and switches channel before you have a chance to object. How do you react?

5. You have just bought a new sweater which you rather like. When you meet up with your friend in a café the next day she notices it straight away and remarks: 'Ouch, that colour doesn't suit you at all.' What do you say in reply?

Compare your answers with the possible ways of responding set out in appendix 2, then move on to section 1, where we start to explore the principal ingredients of acting assertively.

SECTION 1:
ASSERTIVENESS BASICS

---

1. Rights and responsibilities

Many writers and teachers of assertiveness stress the importance of standing up for your own rights whilst also acknowledging the rights and needs of others. In this chapter you will learn about some ideas that you can use to help you to do this.

Reasonableness and respect

Two of the key elements of assertiveness are:

1. Reasonableness
2. Respect

The rights and responsibilities principles that are set out in this chapter are built around these elements. It is important to realize that there are two aspects of showing respect that are relevant to what your rights and responsibilities are. These two aspects are:

1. Showing respect to yourself
2. Showing respect to others

If you act in an overly *aggressive* way then it is likely that you are not showing respect to others. (You may also not be respecting yourself enough to believe that you can act reasonably.)

If you act in an overly *passive* way then it is likely that you are not showing respect to yourself, by not recognizing your own needs or not believing that you have rights. (You may also not be showing respect to others, if your passivity involves you not telling the truth to others or not showing a reasonable level of trust.)

Four 'rights and responsibilities' principles

Below are four principles that are involved in showing respect to others and to yourself which are important to assertiveness. The first three principles are expressed as **rights**. The fourth principle is expressed as a **responsibility**.

1. The right to express your feelings and opinions
   (a) You are entitled to express your feelings and opinions in a reasonable manner.

   (b) Other people are entitled to express their feelings and opinions in a reasonable manner and to be treated with respect.

2. The right to say 'no'
   (a) You are entitled to say 'no' sometimes if you are asked to do something you do not want to do.

(b) Other people are entitled to say 'no' sometimes if you ask them to do something they do not want to do.

3. The right to make mistakes
   (a) It's OK for you to make mistakes sometimes. No one is perfect.

   (b) It's OK for other people to make mistakes sometimes. No one is perfect.

4. The responsibility for making decisions
   (a) You are responsible for making your own decisions – other people do not need to take responsibility for your life.

   (b) Other people are responsible for making their own decisions – you do not need to take responsibility for their lives.

USEFUL TIP If you have a tendency to act too *passively* then focus in particular on the (a) statements in the above principles. You may find it helpful to memorize those and write them out on a card, or pin them on your wall or record them in your mobile phone to remind you of what to focus on. On the other hand, if you have a tendency to act too *aggressively* then memorize and note down the (b) statements above.

Applying the four rights and responsibilities principles

Applying the four rights and responsibilities principles to help you to become more assertive requires you to use them as a benchmark to check whether you are acting assertively, and then to adjust your actions appropriately if you find that you are not following them.

 It is important to exercise some judgement of reasonableness in applying the principles. For example, the first principle says that you can express your feelings and opinions *in a reasonable manner*. You should make your own judgement about what is reasonable in any particular situation.

 Here is an exercise you can try out to help you apply the rights and responsibilities principles.

Exercise 1: Analysing a past situation

Answer the questions below to analyse a past situation where you feel you did not act assertively, either because you were too passive or because you were too aggressive. Repeat the exercise again with another situation if you think it will be helpful.

1. Describe the situation – what happened and what did you do or not do in the situation?

2. What is it that you are not happy with in the way you acted or didn't act in the situation?

3. Consider the four rights and responsibilities principles:

   (a) Right to express your feelings and opinions
   (b) Right to say 'no'
   (c) Right to make mistakes
   (d) Responsibility for making decisions

   Which of the principles seem relevant to this situation?

4. If you accept the four rights and responsibilities principles, what will you do differently the next time a similar situation arises?

5. What can you do to help you carry through your commitment to doing that? (This might include things like reminding yourself of the benefits of doing so, or deciding to reward yourself if you stick to your commitment).

CASE STUDY

Ruth: Analysing a past situation to help exercise your rights

Ruth is someone who tends to act *passively* in her relationship with her partner, Peter. He is quite an assertive person and is comfortable making decisions. Quite often Ruth goes along with this even when she would prefer a different option to the one Peter has chosen. An example of this was recently when they were choosing to go away on holiday with their two young children. Peter suggested they go on a self-catering holiday to keep costs down. Ruth envisaged that doing so would probably leave her doing most of the cooking and any domestic chores while abroad, but she didn't voice her thoughts and indeed that was what ended up happening. She now uses the five-step analysis above to reflect on what happened.

1. Describe the situation – what happened and what did you do or not do in the situation?
'Peter chose for us to go on a self-catering holiday and we ended up doing so, with the result that I did all the cooking and domestic chores and didn't have the break I would have liked.'

2. What is it that you are not happy with in the way you acted or didn't act in the situation?
'I wish I had explained that I didn't want to do all the cooking and chores, and asked him to do a share of them or else arrange for us to have meals out or full board while we were there.'

3. Consider the four rights and responsibilities principles:
(a) *Right to express your feelings and opinions*
(b) *Right to say 'no'*

(c) *Right to make mistakes*
(d) *Responsibility for making decisions*

Which of the principles seem relevant to this situation?
'Principle (a) is most relevant. I didn't explain how I felt or what I wanted in the situation. To some degree (b) was relevant too as I didn't say that I wasn't prepared to do all the cooking/chores, and (d) also applied as I didn't take responsibility for the arrangements but just followed what Peter said despite my reservations.'

If you accept the four rights and responsibilities principles, what will you do differently the next time a similar situation arises?
'Next time I will explain what I would prefer and why. If that leads to a discussion or disagreement, I will then suggest a compromise (for example, if Peter doesn't want to eat out every day because of the cost, I can suggest that we share the burden of the cooking/washing up, etc.).'

What can you do to help you carry through your commitment to doing that?
'Remind myself that at the moment I just fester and feel resentful at having to do all the tasks and that I am unlikely to see a change unless I consciously make an effort to express my views to Peter, because at the moment he is probably unaware of them.'

If you try this exercise and find yourself stuck as to what you can do differently next time the situation arises, look at some of the assertiveness techniques outlined in chapter 3 ('Seven assertiveness techniques') and consider whether any of those might help in your situation.

Exercise 2: Preparing for a future situation
This exercise is similar to the first but it involves preparing for a situation that is likely to happen, rather than a past one. Answer the questions below to prepare for a situation that you know is likely to happen (or that is planned) where you are worried that you might not act assertively, either because you will probably be too aggressive or because you will probably be too passive.

1. Describe the situation – what is likely to happen and what typically might you do or not do?

2. What is it that you are worried about in the way you may act in this situation?

3. Consider the four rights and responsibilities principles:
    (a) Right to express your feelings and opinions
    (b) Right to say 'no'
    (c) Right to make mistakes
    (d) Responsibility for making decisions

    Which of the principles seem relevant to this situation?

4. If you accept the four rights and responsibilities principles, what will you try to do in this situation?

5. What can you do to help you carry through your commitment to trying that?

Jake: Analysing a future situation to help exercise your responsibilities

Jake is someone who tends to act forcefully in exercising his own way but sometimes his forcefulness becomes more like *verbal aggression* or inconsiderateness. Recently he has noticed that in a number of areas where he has been dealing with bureaucratic organizations on the phone, he has lost his patience. He uses exercise 2 to help him reflect on how he might act the next time a similar situation comes up.

1. *Describe the situation – what is likely to happen and what typically might you do or not do?*
   'I get a bill which is inaccurate or a delivery is late, or some other area where an organization I have to deal with does not meet reasonable service standards. I then ring up and complain.'

2. *What is it that you are worried about in the way you may act in this situation?*
   'I am worried that in complaining I become angry and shout or raise my voice at the person on the other end of

the phone, or express my displeasure at the situation in a way which blames the person dealing with the phone call (who probably is not personally at fault). At the end of the day I usually get what I want but later I feel bad about the aggression I showed to the individual.'

3. Consider the four rights and responsibilities principles:
    (a) Right to express your feelings and opinions
    (b) Right to say 'no'
    (c) Right to make mistakes
    (d) Responsibility for making decisions
    Which of the principles seem relevant to this situation?

    'Principle (c) is relevant: if I am too extreme in the way I respond then it's as though I am saying that it's unforgiveable to get something wrong or make a mistake, when actually it happens all the time. Principle (a) is also relevant because by acting in such an aggressive way I am not really respecting the feelings of the person I am talking to.'

4. If you accept the four rights and responsibilities principles, what will you try to do in this situation?
    'I will still explain the issue clearly and make my complaint or request for action to resolve it promptly, but I will do so in a calmer manner and a calmer tone of voice.'

5. *What can you do to help you carry through your commitment to trying that?*
   'Remind myself that if I act in the new way, I will have treated the other person with respect and won't feel so bad afterwards, and that I am just as likely to achieve results.'

Troubleshooting the rights and responsibilities principles

One of the problems that can arise with the rights and responsibilities principles is if you find it difficult to bring yourself to believe that some or all of the four rights and responsibilities principles apply to you.

What can you do if for a long time, perhaps since childhood, you have come to believe that you don't have the right to express your feelings or that you should be perfect and shouldn't make mistakes? These may be longstanding beliefs that you have had instilled in you by important figures such as your parents or others close to you from an early age. Below, **(A)** and **(B)** provide you with two suggestions as to what you can try if this applies to you.

(A) Countering childhood messages that are making it hard for you to be assertive

If you know that there is an explanation in your background or upbringing which explains why you now find it difficult to be assertive – for example, messages you received or things you were told by parents or others when you were young about how you should act – then acknowledging that fact explicitly can help you to move forwards from it. It shows that your difficulties in being assertive are not down to an inherent problem, they are primarily created by messages or ideas you were given by others or by events. One way to improve your assertiveness is consciously to start countering those messages, that internal negative dialogue, with new, more constructive messages. The **positive message** exercise below is a way of helping you to do that.

---

1. Are there any features in your personal background which you think might give an explanation of why you have difficulty in being assertive? These might be, for example, expectations or pressures that your parents, siblings or teachers placed on you when you were young. They could also be cultural or gender-based ideas you have taken from society or from people close to you about how you should or should not act. Complete the sentence below giving a simple explanation for why you might have difficulty in acting assertively, referring to those features.

   'I sometimes have difficulty in acting assertively because ...'

2. Looking at what you have written, what can you say to challenge the features in your background that you

have highlighted? What can you say to argue that they do not have to be correct and that you can, with practice, overcome them and act more assertively? For example, if your answer to question 1 was 'I sometimes have difficulty in acting assertively because when I was young I was taught that "Girls should be seen and not heard" by my mother', you might challenge this by writing down: 'Women have as much right to express their views as men. My mother had her own opinions and I do not need to agree to them. It may take time but I am going to try to start expressing my own view more and see what happens ...'

Create your own **positive challenge** to the explanation you gave in question 1. Try to create a challenge which you personally will find motivating and encouraging. (It need not be identical or even similar to the example given – what is important is that it is meaningful and positive for you.)

3. If your confidence starts to waver, remind yourself of the positive message that you stated in question 2. Use it as a motivating force to help you try out more assertive actions when you can. If helpful, read through the statement you made in question 2 every day, or put it somewhere where you can refer to it whenever you want and use it to encourage yourself.

CASE STUDY

Ruth (continued): Creating a positive challenge to a negative childhood message

Working through the above exercise, Ruth realizes that her habit of not expressing her views and feelings stems from her childhood, when she tended to play second fiddle to her older sister, Debbie, who was always much more vocal, tending to take the initiative in conversations and criticize Ruth if she started to express views that Debbie disagreed with. Ruth creates her own positive challenge to this negative message:

'I sometimes have difficulty in acting assertively because of the way Debbie criticized me when we were children, but I am older now and as an adult can make my own decisions and express my own opinions. Just because Debbie criticized me when we were children doesn't mean that everyone else will now, and even if they do I still have a right to express my own opinion.'

To help get her viewpoint and feelings across, Ruth reminds herself of this positive message when she is tempted not to speak up for herself in conversations with others.

Some people find that it is helpful to express the positive challenge they have created to a childhood message in the second person ('you') form, rather than the first person ('I') form. You can experiment with both ways and see which works best for you. If Ruth had expressed her positive challenge in the second person, she might have worded it like this:

> 'You sometimes have difficulty in acting assertively because when you were younger you were criticized for doing so by your sister, but now you are an adult you can make your own decisions and express your own opinions. Just because Debbie criticized you when you were young doesn't mean that everyone else will now, and even if they do you still have a right to express your own opinion.'

(B) Focusing on outcomes

If you are continually thinking about what you *ought* to do or what is *right* for you to do in a particular kind of situation, then this can exert considerable pressure on you and create stress. When you catch yourself doing this, one thing you can do is to focus instead on what *outcomes* you want to achieve from a situation. The exercise that follows is a simple way of encouraging you to do this. Instead of focusing on your moral messages about what you *should* do, answer the questions below to help you focus on what *outcomes* you want to achieve from the situation.

---

1. Describe a situation where you are unsure about how to act, or find yourself thinking that you *should* or *ought* to act in a certain way.

2. What *outcomes* do you want to achieve from the situation?

3. List some different options for how you might act in the situation and comment on how well they will contribute towards achieving the outcomes that you want.

4. In light of your consideration of options, which option do you want to try out?

5. On a scale of 0–10 (where 10 is a certainty), how likely do you think it is that you will try out the option you have stated in question 4?

6. If your score for likelihood in question 5 is less than 8, what can you do to bring it up by one or more points, i.e. what can you do to make it a little more likely that you will try out the proposed action? For example, this might include enlisting support in some way or making a written reminder or promising yourself a simple reward if you do manage to try out the action.

Jake (continued): Focusing on outcomes you want

Jake realizes that part of the reason that he has a tendency to speak aggressively when challenging poor service standards is that his self-esteem would suffer if his challenge were unsuccessful. He feels that he *ought* to make it absolutely clear to the people he is talking to that their service standards are unacceptable and that if he doesn't manage to get the organization to admit its error, then he will view himself as a bit inadequate or incompetent. This prospect is worrying to him, so he tends to overcompensate and speak too loudly or use language which is very severe, in the belief that this will make it more likely for him to get what he wants. On going through the above exercise, focusing on *outcomes*, Jake realizes that there are two outcomes he wants from the situation: the first is to get a practical result from the conversation (for the issue he is complaining about to be resolved to his satisfaction) and the second is for him to feel relaxed after the conversation. He realizes that making his point clearly and calmly is just as likely to achieve the practical result he wants as making it aggressively, and it is more likely to leave him feeling relaxed after the conversation than if he shouts or blames. This reinforces his intention to try the new, calmer approach next time. He rates the likelihood of him doing that as 7 out of 10 and decides to tell his partner that he intends to do that. His partner, who recognizes that he can sometimes be quite verbally aggressive, supports the idea and this helps him to gain the confidence and commitment to try it out.

The four exercises described in this chapter for helping you to make use of the rights and responsibilities principles (analysing a past situation; preparing for a future situation;

creating a positive message to counter childhood messages; focusing on outcomes) can all be used, whether or not your tendency is to be passive or assertive in a particular situation. The answers you get may be different in nature depending on whether your natural inclination is to be too passive or too assertive, but they will be appropriate for you and your situation.

The importance of patience

Learning to become more assertive is like learning a new language, new ways of acting or new habits. Be patient with yourself. Like learning any new skills, language or habit, this takes time and practice. Because the habit of not being assertive and the underlying beliefs that go with that habit have been with you for a long time, at first the process of retraining yourself into new, more productive habits may seem unnatural or difficult, or you may lapse into old habits at times. This is normal. Give yourself credit for times that you succeed in being more assertive than you would have been before. If you slip up at any point, rather than being overly self-critical, adopt a practical viewpoint: ask yourself if there is anything you can learn from the slip-up and then try to get back on track.

Key ideas from chapter 1

From the ideas in chapter 1, try in particular to remember that:

- Standing up for rights involves giving yourself and others a reasonable level of respect

- In situations where you have a tendency to be passive, focus in particular on the (a) formulations of the four rights and responsibilities principles (pp. 14–15)

- In situations where you have a tendency to be aggressive, focus in particular on the (b) formulations of the four rights and responsibilities principles (pp. 14–15)

- Try applying the rights and responsibilities principles by completing *Exercise 1 – Analysing a past situation* (pp. 16–17) or *Exercise 2 – Preparing for a future situation* (pp. 20–21). If you find it difficult to see the principles as applying to you, then apply the troubleshooting techniques (p. 23ff).

2. Communicating effectively

At the heart of being assertive is the ability to communicate effectively with people. In this chapter we consider four key aspects of effective personal communication and give ideas for practising each aspect with a view to helping you build your skills in expressing yourself and engaging in constructive and productive conversations with other people, even on difficult topics.

The elements of communication described in this chapter may not *always* help you. For example, if you are faced with someone who is acting in a highly manipulative way you may need to try some of the more specific advanced techniques covered in chapter 3. However, the aspects covered here are important primary communication skills that it is helpful to be aware of and to develop. If some of them seem obvious or simple to you, then it is still worth remembering that sometimes when things aren't working well in a relationship or dialogue, going back to these basics of communication can be helpful. The four primary elements of communication covered in this chapter are:

1. Listening effectively
2. Developing conversations
3. Expressing yourself
4. Negotiating effectively

1. Listening effectively

The first step to being able to communicate well is to learn how to listen effectively. There are a number of reasons why listening effectively can actually help you to express yourself and be more effective in getting across your own viewpoints and wishes.

If you show people that you have really heard what they are saying:

- They are more likely to pay attention to your comments than if they think you are not listening or have misunderstood them

- They are more likely to feel positive towards you than if you have shown no sensitivity to what they have said

- They are more likely to open up to you and disclose relevant information about themselves or whatever you are discussing.

If you actively listen to what people say:

- You are more likely to avoid misunderstandings that could lead you to jump to inaccurate conclusions

- You are more likely to gain appropriate insight into what they are thinking and feeling, so as to be able to respond to them better

- You are more likely to gain clarity about those aspects of what they are saying that you agree with and those

33

aspects that you disagree with, so that you can know when to support and when to challenge.

Ingredients of good listening

When communicating with someone you can help to gain their respect and attention by showing that you are listening to them through:

- Giving your full attention and not looking away or allowing distractions to interrupt the conversation

- Focusing yourself on what the other person is saying – if your mind starts to wander try to bring it back and refocus on what they are communicating to you

- Letting the other person finish what they are saying before you speak

- Asking appropriate questions to clarify anything they are saying which you are not sure you have understood

- Showing you are paying attention by your body language, for example, by responding with nods of the head, sounds of agreement or facial expressions indicating an alert response and attention

- Commenting on what they are saying in a constructive, positive way when appropriate, with comments that show you have listened (e.g. by picking up on specific points they have made).

Three core listening skills

Three core listening skills worth practising are:

(i) **Paraphrasing** – reframing what someone has said to you in a way that captures the essence of it without being a verbatim repeat of it, e.g.

> *Other person's statement:* 'Ever since I had the accident I have found I need much more sleep.'

> *Paraphrase:* 'The accident has left you really tired.'

(ii) **Summarizing** – feeding back the main points in what someone has said., e.g.

> *Other person's statement:* 'To get to the motorway, go left out of the door along Acacia Avenue, over the traffic lights, down the hill, along St James' Street then right at the T-junction and follow the road up for about ten minutes until you get to the motorway junction.'

> *Summarizing:* 'Left, through the lights, down the hill then right.'

(iii) **Reflecting** – showing that you understand the significance of what someone is saying to you, e.g.

> *Other person's statement:* 'When the children went to university I spent a lot of the day not knowing what to do and just tried to get on with routine tasks.'

Reflection: 'When the children went to university it left a gap in your life.'

---

2. Developing conversations

If you can increase your ability to put other people at their ease and to talk about yourself in a relaxed way, this will have benefits in a number of settings and is likely to help you to:

- Build positive relationships

- Come across as confident and assertive

- Create an environment of mutual interest and respect in which it is easier to broach difficult topics or express personal views, because the groundwork of good communication already exists.

Key terms: Free information and self-disclosure

Following up on free information and providing *self-disclosure* are ways of helping to develop relaxed and balanced communication, highlighted by Manuel Smith in his book *When I Say No, I Feel Guilty* (Mass Market Paperback, 1975). Following up on free information involves asking interested questions or making comments that demonstrate interest when someone tells you something about themselves that they don't have to (i.e. when they give you 'free information' about themselves).

Self-disclosure is when *you* freely disclose something about *yourself* (either in response to some free information from the other person in a balanced conversation, or else in developing a social exchange with someone). In cases where you don't know the person particularly well, the kind of following up of free information and disclosure about yourself that we are looking at is usually nothing *too* personal but acts as a kind of invitation to a conversation or encouragement to *continue* a conversation.

For example, if you ask someone, 'Do you live near here?', and they respond with a simple 'yes' or a simple 'no', they have not given you any other information than a strict response to your question. However, if they respond by saying 'Yes, I live two blocks down near the shopping centre', or 'No, I live in Westfield-Under-Edge. I'm just down here visiting my sister', then they have given you some free information.

You could of course simply ignore the free information they have given you, but if you want to develop the conversation in a balanced way, then it is usually helpful to respond to their piece of free information either by a simple follow-up inquiry, such as: 'How do you find it being so close to the shops?' or 'Do you enjoy shopping?', or by disclosing some personal information about yourself (nothing too significant in an initial exchange), e.g. 'I'm not sure I could cope with being so near to a shopping centre – it might do serious damage to my credit card.'

REMEMBER THIS!!! If you can get into the habit of using the conversational skills of following up on free information and disclosing information about yourself in a relatively *low-key*, balanced way, it will help to lay the groundwork for more advanced communication and to convey an impression of you as being relaxed and confident in talking with others.

If you want to encourage someone to expand on a topic or personal view or experience, it can be useful to use *open questions*: questions which do not point them to a specific conclusion or a 'yes' or 'no' answer, but instead leave it up to them to develop their response in the way that they want. Examples of open questions are questions beginning with any of the following phrases:

- 'What do you think of ...?'
- 'What are your views on ...?'
- 'How do you feel about ...?'

3. Expressing yourself

(i) Taking ownership of your own feelings, thoughts and opinions

A lot of advice about assertiveness stresses that speaking in an assertive way involves taking ownership of your own feelings, thoughts and opinions. This involves:

- Using **'I' statements** to express your own views or feelings, such as:
    - 'I would like it if ...'
    - 'I prefer ...'
    - 'I think ...'
    - 'I feel ...'

- Making it clear when you are stating an opinion or personal viewpoint, for example using phrases such as:
  - 'In my opinion ...'
  - 'My personal view is that ...'
  - 'My impression is that ...'

Reasons why this can be helpful

If you get into the habit of expressing your personal views in this way:

- It can remind you that you have the *right* to express your views. This can help you to feel more confident

- It can make it clear to the person you are speaking to that you are acknowledging a *personal opinion* or *personal view*, not pretending to state an objective truth nor insisting that they must hold the same view or feel the same way. This helps the other person to feel that you are not being dogmatic but are simply being open about what you think or feel.

 Over the next day, make a mental note of the number of times in which you make a personal observation or express a personal view *without* expressing it in an 'I' statement, and without acknowledging it as your own experience or comment. On the following day, consciously try to use the 'I' statement format or phrases to make it clear that you are giving a personal viewpoint and not claiming a universal truth. See if you notice any difference in the reactions of the people you are with and observe how you feel when you do this. If you are good friends with any of the people you speak to during this day of owning your personal views and feelings, then you could also ask them for their views or responses to you speaking in that way.

REMEMBER THIS!!! While owning your personal views and feelings can be very helpful, it can also sometimes be taken too far. There are a number of situations in which it is obvious, from the mere fact that it is you who are speaking, that what you are doing is expressing your own views or feelings, so that using 'I' statements can be a bit artificial. You may end up sounding like someone who is just repeating an assertiveness technique rather than genuinely owning your own feelings! While for most people who are not usually particularly assertive, consciously practising the use of 'I' statements for expressing your feelings and opinions is a sensible and useful thing to do, over time it would be better to make your own judgement about the extent to which you want to do that, and be aware of occasions when it may be found a bit artificial or pompous.

(ii) Common elements of expressing yourself assertively

Here are some do's and don'ts worth remembering for when you want to express yourself assertively. These are guiding principles rather than hard and fast rules. You may be able to find particular situations where there is a reason to vary from them but for most situations they will help you to communicate effectively.

You should **try to**:

- Be clear in saying what you want and how you feel

- Stay calm and speak calmly

- Keep steady eye contact (unless you are in a situation where this would cause offence for cultural reasons) but do not stare

- Give others the opportunity to express their views and feelings.

You should **try not to**:

- Apologize excessively or overjustify your actions or decisions

- Speak in roundabout or indirect ways

- Make vague or implied criticisms

- Make commitments that you cannot keep

- Shout or invade someone else's personal space.

(iii) Assertive body language

Assertive people tend to show by their facial expressions, gestures, posture and movements that they are confident and relaxed without being aggressive. Aspects of assertive body language may include:

- Using a range of facial expressions in appropriate ways matching how you are feeling and thinking (e.g. smiling if you are happy, furrowing your brows and narrowing your eyes if you are angry, raising your eyebrows if you are questioning, opening your eyes wide if you are surprised)

- Gesturing in relaxed ways with your hands to give emphasis and animation (this should not be confused with pointing at someone you are talking to, which is generally an aggressive form of behaviour)

- Keeping an appropriate distance for the kind of communication and relationship you are in (for example, if you do not know someone well then getting too close to them can be intimidating, but on the other hand if you stay *too* far away from someone, it can be a sign that you are nervous or anxious)

- Being comfortable in both leading and following others rather than always wanting to lose yourself in a crowd, or always taking an overly domineering approach and insisting on always being at the front.

Perhaps the most important element in relation to your body language if you want to be assertive is to *be aware* of how you are acting and coming across, and what facial expressions or bodily movements you are adopting. Sometimes, simply becoming aware that your body is tense or that you are raising your voice inappropriately (or alternatively speaking so quietly that it is difficult for others to hear you) can be enough to enable you to change your behaviour.

 The next time you are in a conversation with someone, consciously reflect on how your body is feeling, how you are standing or sitting, any gestures you are or are not making and the volume and sound of your voice. If you feel that there is anything in your body language which might come across as being unduly passive (or alternatively as being inappropriately aggressive), then try to change it consciously so that your body language becomes more assertive. Afterwards reflect on how you felt after changing your behaviour and whether the other person reacted differently to you. (As with the exercise on 'I' statements (pp. 40–41), if you know them well enough you might afterwards ask them if they noticed the change in behaviour and whether they have any feedback about it to give you.)

(iv) Expressing criticism

If someone does something that you don't like, there is little point in simply criticizing them in a negative way as this may well simply make them upset or angry. You are usually more likely to produce the results you would like if you give them *constructive criticism*, i.e. you indicate what you would like them to do differently, so that they can then see a way forward if they want to take it.

'The accounts you prepared don't balance' would be an example of criticism that is simply negative.

'Unfortunately, the accounts you prepared don't balance. Could you have another look at the calculations you did about the managing agent's fees – I think that's where the error occurred', would be an example of criticism that is more constructive because it shows the person what they can do to remedy the problem.

Key term: The assertion sandwich

One technique that you can use to try to make criticism produce more positive results, as well as make it more palatable for the person receiving it, is to put your criticism in a 'sandwich' between two positive points. Combining this approach with the idea of making your criticism constructive, you can create an assertion sandwich that has the following ingredients:

1. An initial **positive** comment or piece of praise *followed by* …

2. A **negative** comment with a constructive suggestion *followed by* ...

3. A second **positive** comment

Adapting the previous example, your assertion sandwich might be something like:

> 'Thanks for preparing the information about the rental of the property. I've now got a better idea of how it all works *[initial positive comment]*. Unfortunately the accounts you prepared don't balance *[negative comment]*. Could you have another look at the calculations you did about the managing agent's fees – I think that's where the error occurred *[constructive suggestion]*. That's the only thing I could find that needs adjustment. Overall, I really like the way you've set it out – it's excellent *[second positive comment]*.'

(v) Challenging others

Some people worry a great deal about how best to challenge people if they disagree with them or don't like something they have done or are planning to do. In later chapters we will consider how best to deal with any *thought patterns* that might be making it difficult for you to challenge others, such as worries about what the other person may think of you (see chapter 4). Here are two initial suggestions about constructive ways of challenging others.

(a) Comment on the action rather than on the person's character

If possible, when you don't like something someone has done or is intending to do, comment specifically on their action rather than make a generalized comment which is an attack on their character or on them as a person, e.g. 'You quite often arrive late' would be more constructive than 'You are unreliable' – the former focuses on specific actions or behaviour, rather than on a claimed character trait.

'I think that sometimes you could express yourself more sensitively' would be more constructive than 'You have no feelings.' It is less extreme and, again, it describes behaviour which could be open to change rather than on a presumed permanent character defect. It also uses an 'I' statement which makes it clear that this is a personal view and that others may disagree.

(b) Roll with resistance

Roll with resistance is an approach used in 'motivational interviewing', a model for helping to motivate people to change problematic behaviour patterns devised by William R Miller and Stephen Rollnick. The approach is explained in their book *Motivational Interviewing: Helping People Change* (3rd Edition 2012).

Rolling with resistance can be helpful when another person is repeatedly doing something that is creating problems for them, for you or for others and they don't seem to be acknowledging any need for change (or else they deny that they *can* change). It involves not challenging the other person directly in a head-on confrontation, which may just meet with further denial, resistance or attack, but instead using your listening skills to encourage them to explain and clarify their thoughts and feelings, and then getting them to draw out for themselves the implications of their actions, the possible options open to them and the consequences of each option. Quite often when you use this kind of approach, the other person may of their own accord come up with constructive suggestions about how they can try to act that chime with your own views, whereas if you had lectured them on those very same options you might have met with denial or further resistance!

If you want to try out challenging someone whose behaviour is creating problems by using the roll with resistance approach, then one way you can do it is by following a two-step process.

Step 1: Use your listening skills

Use the listening skills described earlier in this chapter to encourage the other person to explain what they are thinking and feeling about the situation. For example, you could paraphrase, summarize or reflect it back to them in a way that shows that you have heard what they are saying, even if you don't agree with it. Do this in a non-judgmental way: the primary aim is to show that you are listening to them and to encourage exploration of possible solutions in a constructive way.

If they are in part aware that what they are saying or doing is unreasonable, then simply hearing what they are saying relayed back to them without being overtly attacked may prompt them to acknowledge issues and think about how to make changes. Remember that they may be expecting you to criticize them, so a simple restatement of their views may disarm them and encourage them to think and act more constructively. Once they have explained what they think and feel you can encourage them to think about possible solutions with you.

Step 2: Develop discrepancy

After you have reflected back to the other person what they are saying about their behaviour, ask them in a non-confrontational way how their views, comments or actions fit in with wider goals or objectives if it appears that there is a discrepancy (i.e. if it appears that their actions are at odds with what they want to achieve).

Lucy and Vince: Rolling with resistance to encourage constructive change

Lucy and Vince are a couple who have been having some difficulties in their relationship. They seem to spend a lot of their time bickering about minor issues, and the romance of the early period of their relationship seems, for the moment, a thing of the distant past. A few weeks ago they had a conversation about some

of the difficulties and both agreed to try harder to communicate better with each other and to try to get back some
of the harmony they had in the relationship previously. For
a couple of days this went well but then they had an argument and since then Vince has been going out most nights
with his friends and coming back late, so they have spent
little time together and only communicated cursorily. One
day after they have both finished work and are eating dinner together at home, Lucy raises the issue with Vince. She
consciously uses the roll with resistance approach to try to
encourage Vince to talk constructively about this.

Lucy: 'Are you going out tonight?'
Vince: 'Yes, I've arranged to see Trevor and Mark at 8.30pm
    – is there anything wrong with that?' [defensive, resistant
    comment]
Lucy: 'No – it's good if you want to spend some time with
    your friends. I just wondered, is there a particular reason?'
    [inviting further comment without judgement rather than
    challenging in a confrontational way]
Vince: 'Well, I know I can just relax and be myself if I'm out
    with friends.'
Lucy: 'You're feeling you can't really relax if you're back
    here with me in the evening?' [reflecting back]
Vince: 'Well, since we had that argument, I didn't think it
    would be a great idea for us to be together too much
    in the evening' [opening up and explaining his concerns]

Lucy: 'You thought we might just start arguing again?' *[summarizing/reflecting]*

Vince: 'Yes, I didn't want that.'

Lucy: 'I see what you mean, but if we hardly see each other at all how does that fit in with trying to communicate better?' *[indicating the discrepancy between Vince's behaviour and their previous joint goal]*

Vince: 'It doesn't really I suppose, only I'm worried that we might just start arguing again if I stay in.' *[responding without defensiveness, explaining his concern]*

Lucy: 'What could we do that might help us to avoid arguing and communicate better?' *[inviting exploration of solutions in a collaborative, non-aggressive way]*

Vince: 'Maybe we could agree to do something together two or three times a week which we discuss together first and leave the other evenings free to go out on our own, so that we have some space but also some time together to try to get back to where we were?' *[constructive response]*

Lucy: 'OK, I'd like that, what days do you suggest?'

Vince: 'I don't know – maybe if we do it on a week by week basis – how about if we keep Wednesday evening and Saturday free next week and try to do something together then?'

Lucy: 'Yes I'd like that, let's try that for a start.'

Think of a situation you are in where you and the other person have a mutual interest in making progress and getting on, but the other person seems to be acting in a way which makes that difficult. Try using the roll with resistance approach to show them that you are paying attention to how they think and feel and to encourage them to think of constructive changes that might be in both your interests.

4. Negotiating effectively

In some situations you may want to do more than simply challenge another person or encourage them to make changes of their own accord. There are times when other people will only make adjustments to their behaviour if they are persuaded that making the adjustments will be preferable for them to not doing so. In these kinds of situation, you may have to *negotiate* changes with them. There may also be times when demands or requests are being placed on you by others, which you do not wish to meet or feel that it is unreasonable to expect you to meet. Again, in those situations you may well find that in order for you to resist the demands or to persuade the other person to withdraw or modify them, what you need is negotiating skills. Here are fifteen tips for negotiating a change in someone else's behaviour or resisting an unreasonable demand that is being placed on you.

15 Negotiation tips

Depending on the situation you find yourself in, some of the tips below may be more useful or relevant than others. Reflect on which are likely to be most helpful in your particular situation and make use of those.

1. Before you speak to the other person, if possible, clarify for yourself what outcome you would like to achieve from the negotiation or discussion you are going to have.

2. Identify for yourself what things you are prepared to compromise on and what things you are not willing to compromise on because they are too important to you.

3. In light of your knowledge of the behaviour and personality of the person you are going to be in discussion or negotiation with, give some thought in advance to what they might ask for or say when you raise the issue and how you might respond.

4. Be prepared to listen to what the other person has to say but also think about how you are going to ensure that you get an opportunity to put your point of view and feelings across.

5. Prepare for how you may try to move the discussion forward once you have both expressed your views.

6. In respect of those aspects where you might compromise, think of possible suggestions that you might make to the other party about what you would like *in return* from them if you compromise on those aspects.

7. In respect of those aspects where you are *not* willing to compromise, be clear in your own mind about what the consequences might be if the other person still refuses to meet those 'bottom-line' requests and what you will then do.

8. If your bottom-line requests are not met, then be prepared to act in the way you decided beforehand (in tip 7). If you are not prepared to carry through this commitment, then you may decide that what you considered to be a 'non-negotiable' or bottom-line request is actually just a strong preference. It is best to be clear about this in your own mind beforehand, if possible.

9. In light of your relationship with the other party and your knowledge of them, give some thought in advance to *what style of approach* is most likely to encourage the other party to respond positively to your request. Will it help for you to be encouraging and constructive and try to engage in a joint search for solutions, or will it be more likely to be productive if you take a firm stance from the outset, indicating clearly what you want and how you will act if your wishes are not met? The best

style of approach may vary for different situations and different people.

10. *When, where* and *how* do you want to approach the topic to give yourself the best chance of getting a friendly, constructive or at least helpful response from the other party? In most cases you may want to raise the subject at a time when both you and the other party can give full attention to the discussion without distractions, and when you are not preoccupied with other matters or very tired or stressed.

11. While you are looking for a good time to raise the topic, as indicated in tip 10, don't put off the moment forever! The perfect time will probably never happen. If you find yourself delaying too much, then select a specific time or occasion to raise the matter and keep to your commitment.

12. Recognize that the person you are going to be talking to may say some things that you are not anticipating. If you are worried about committing yourself to something that you will later regret, then prepare a stock response for the unexpected which will allow you time to think further before you make a decision, e.g. something as simple as: 'I need to think about that before I give you my answer.'

13. When you have considered all the above points, write down a summary of your thoughts and go through it

before you speak with the other person so that you are prepared.

14. When you speak with the person, if you do both agree a way of moving forward, then confirm exactly what you have agreed at the end of the discussion to avoid any possible misunderstanding. Depending on the situation, it may also be appropriate to make a written note of what you have agreed and share that with them afterwards so that you have a point of reference.

15. If appropriate, decide how you both are going to keep track of whether the agreed actions have been implemented and what you would both regard as successful implementation. If appropriate, set a provisional date for a further discussion to review progress and to discuss whether the agreement has worked or needs to be changed.

 Reflect on a past situation where you would have liked to have persuaded someone to do something (or to stop doing something) and you raised it with them but did not have any success. Read through the above negotiation tips and think about which of them might have helped you to achieve a better result. Bear those in mind for future use if you find yourself in a similar situation. If helpful, write them down for reference.

Key ideas from chapter 2

From the ideas in chapter 2, bear in mind that:

- Listening effectively is the first step to communicating effectively

- You can use the techniques of following up on free information and self-disclosure (p. 37) to help you build relaxed conversations

- Take ownership of your feelings, thoughts and opinions by using 'I' statements (p. 39)

- Try using an 'assertion sandwich' (p. 45) to criticize someone constructively

- Consider 'rolling with resistance' rather than head-on confrontation as a way of challenging people (p. 47)

- Where a stronger approach is required make use of negotiation tips (pp. 53–56).

3. Seven assertiveness techniques

In this chapter we look at seven standard assertiveness techniques that you can try out, illustrating them with case studies. The techniques can be very helpful in the right situations and in giving you a guideline as to what to try if what you are doing isn't working. However, it is important to realize that they will not be appropriate for you in every case. For example, if you are in a situation where there is a power imbalance and the other person holds all the power (if, for instance, they are in a position of authority at work), then it is sometimes better to hold your tongue rather than to speak assertively.

 If you are in any doubt as to whether to try out one of the assertiveness techniques in your situation, then weigh up the likelihood of it producing a helpful result and the potential benefit of that against the likelihood and seriousness of the potential downside if it doesn't work. If the downside is small or is only likely to be temporary, then it may well be worth taking the risk of trying to be assertive, but if the downside is high then you may want to think carefully and perhaps seek someone else's view before going ahead with your assertive action.

In the case studies provided for each technique you can see examples of situations where the techniques can be very helpful, together with tips as to how to implement them.

1. Saying 'no'

Many people find it hard to refuse a request or resist pressure to do something. The following are **key points to remember in saying 'no'**:

- Be clear and explicit in refusal

- Be polite but firm

- If the other person asks for reasons or seeks to extend the conversation, keep your explanations to an absolute minimum or simply ignore the request and repeat your refusal. You do not need to justify yourself just because they ask you to!

- After you have repeated your polite refusal one or more times, indicate that you are now going to end the conversation and do so in an active way (e.g. by closing the door, as in the case study below, or by putting the phone down on a phone call, having indicated politely that you are going to do so)

- If you are in a face-to-face situation where ending the conversation by closing a door is not possible, then end it in another way, e.g. by moving out of the room or by simply not responding to further comments or changing the subject to something you are happy to talk about (after you have told the other person you are going to do that)

- If possible, practise saying 'no' first in a situation where the potential problems for you if it doesn't work out are minimal (such as the door-to-door salesperson situation in the case study below, or when dealing with a marketing call on the phone). Once you have had some success in this, you can move on to situations involving someone you know on a professional or personal level.

Guy: Saying 'no'

Guy is at home with his two children when the doorbell rings. He answers it to find a man and a woman on his doorstep who want to request a donation from him towards the children's charity that they represent. Guy annually gives donations to two charities of his own choosing and he sometimes responds to appeals in relation to special crises or disasters, but he doesn't really like to give donations to charities on his doorstep and he is also busy when these representatives call. However, normally he finds it difficult to say 'no' and he often ends up in extended conversations in this kind of situation which might finish with him donating something or else feeling guilty for not doing so. Recently, he has made a conscious decision to keep conversations brief with people who are cold-calling or approaching him on the doorstep, and to make it clear as concisely as possible that he is declining to take up their offer while still being polite. On this occasion, the conversation goes as follows once he has opened the door:

Female charity representative (smiling): 'Hello sir, we are in the area to let people know about the good work being done by [a children's charity] all over the world to help sick children. In the last month alone, the society has enabled over 200,000 children worldwide to recover from or cope with the symptoms of disabling conditions or malnutrition through the provision of simple life-saving advice and dietary supplements. Our information pack details the different services that are provided and the huge difference that it makes to young children and their families.' (She holds out a large information pack towards Guy.)

Guy (holding up his hand to decline the offer of the information pack): 'Thank you, but I'm not interested.' (He puts his hand on the door and starts to turn to go.) *[explicit polite refusal accompanied by accompanying movement away]*

Male charity representative (interjecting): 'Can I ask what your reason is? We have a wide variety of different options and we could give you some information just to show you a bit more about the work.'

Guy: 'Thank you but I'm not interested.' *[repeated firm, clear, polite refusal]*

Female charity representative (displaying her identity badge): 'In case you are worried that we might not be genuine, you can see our identity badges here. Do you donate to any charities at the moment?'

Guy: 'Thank you but I'm not interested in your service. I don't mean to be rude but I'm going to shut the door now.' (He shuts the door and goes back into his house) [*polite refusal, ignoring attempt to draw him into the conversation and moving out of the situation to avoid further discussion*]

Saying 'no' to someone you know well

For many people, saying 'no' is much harder when you are talking to someone you know well such as a friend or partner. There are obvious reasons why you might find this more difficult:

- You are likely to be more worried about offending or upsetting your friend or partner than you might be about refusing a request from someone you don't know and therefore don't have an emotional connection with

- Unlike with someone you may never see again, with someone you know well, you may be worried that saying 'no' could damage your relationship and lead to adverse consequences for you in the future. In fact, in many situations, giving an ambiguous response may be more likely to lead to frustration or difficulties in your relationship with someone you know than giving a clear 'no'. Always saying 'yes' may also lose you respect in the other person's eyes. However, it is true that saying 'no' to someone you know well *may* have consequences in your relationship with them, and it is sensible to try to do your best to increase the chances of those consequences being *positive* rather than negative. Therefore, in saying 'no' to someone you know well, I would suggest that you try to observe the following adapted key tips for saying 'no'.

Key points to remember in saying 'no' to someone you know well

- Remember that it can be frustrating or annoying for others if you are ambiguous in what you say, or if you do not carry through what you say. Where you are asked to do something by someone you know well (and want to maintain a positive relationship with), it is therefore particularly important to **be honest and clear** in saying 'no' to requests that you cannot carry out, or that you don't need to agree to and don't want to agree to

- **Be polite** – if you lose control and start shouting at someone or behaving aggressively in other ways or sulking, then this puts the relationship under pressure. It is normally better to express what you are saying in a reasonable and polite way if you can remember to do so, though this may take some effort and you may not always be able to achieve it, particularly in the heat of the moment!

- If you are not sure about whether or not you will agree to the request, then in most cases explain that to the other person – usually you don't have to make an instant decision. If necessary, you can explain to the other person that you will *give it some thought* and let them know. (If you postpone the decision in this way, then be sure that you do subsequently let them know instead of leaving your answer in the air indefinitely!)

- **Consider a compromise *if appropriate*** – if you are not very keen on carrying out the request but would be willing to do so if it were modified or if the other person were to do something in return for you, then consider offering an alternative suggestion or compromise. (Later on, we will explore what is involved in offering a compromise as an assertiveness technique in its own right). If on reflection, however, you decide that a compromise would *not* be appropriate, then don't feel that you *always* have to compromise. Sometimes you may reach a point where you don't think compromise would be sensible or helpful and, if that is so, remain firm and communicate that to the other person

- **Give a simple explanation of your reasons for not acceding to the request but don't overdo it!** When you are dealing with a stranger there may be no need to explain your reasons for refusing a request. For example, in the previous case study involving Guy and the door-to-door charity representatives, Guy said that he was not interested. In that situation there was no need for him to explain further. In the case of refusing a request from someone you know, however, the situation is slightly different. If you want to maintain good communication with the person you are speaking to, then it will usually help them to understand where you are coming from if you give a simple explanation of the reason for your refusal. It is important, however, not to overdo that explanation. A short simple explanation is usually more effective than multiple or extended explanations, which often convey the impression that you are trying to justify yourself and can reduce the clarity of your message

- **Don't give in to unreasonable emotional pressure!**
  If the other person starts trying to make you feel guilty for something that's not your responsibility, don't give in – maintain your polite refusal. Remind yourself of the reasons why you are saying 'no', if you find this difficult.

Paula and Jasmine: Saying 'no' to someone you know well

Paula and Jasmine are good friends and live a few doors down from each other in the same street. They have children of similar ages who go to the same school. Often they make arrangements to help each other out with childcare arrangements. One Friday, Paula rings Jasmine up in the morning and asks her if she would be able to collect Paula's eight-year-old daughter Philippa for her the following day from a drama group that Philippa goes to on Saturdays. After an initial preliminary conversation, Paula makes her request.

Paula: 'I wonder if you could do me a favour. Philippa's got her drama group tomorrow morning. I've just realized I've got to be in between 12 and 2pm tomorrow to receive a delivery, so it's unlikely I'll be able to collect her at 2pm when the class ends. Do you think you could collect her for me? It would be really helpful.'

Jasmine: [politely and clearly explaining that she may not be able to do it and the reason] 'That's the time that I normally do my homework for my German evening class, so I don't think I'll be able to help out this time I'm afraid.'

Paula: 'Would it be possible for you to do the homework another time? I'm really stuck and it would be very helpful if you could do it for me?'

Jasmine: [clearly stating her position but also allowing time to reflect] 'I don't think that's going to be possible I'm afraid, but I'll give it a bit of thought and get back to you early this afternoon to let you know for certain whether or not I can.'

Paula: 'Thanks. I'd be ever so grateful if you could.'

Jasmine: [repeating that she will reflect but not committing beyond that] 'OK, I'll think about it. I don't think I will be able to but I'll let you know.'

After the phone conversation, Jasmine reflects on the situation. She realizes that doing her preparation for her German class at another time will actually be quite difficult for her because of other commitments, so she decides that she will tell Paula clearly that she can't do it. She calls Paula back and explains briefly:

Jasmine: [indicating politely that she is refusing the request and giving a simple explanation] 'Hi Paula, I've had a further think about Saturday morning, but I'm afraid it would be too difficult for me to rearrange doing my German homework because I've got other commitments. I'm sorry I'm not going to be able to help you with this one.'
Paula: 'Oh dear, that's going to put me in some difficulty, can't you rearrange some of the other things?'
Jasmine: [remaining firm and not giving in to emotional pressure] 'I'm sorry but that would be too difficult. I hope you find a way of sorting it out.'
Paula: 'I don't know if I will but thanks anyway.'

Looking at the above dialogue you can see that Paula has put a lot of emotional pressure on Jasmine, by suggesting that if Jasmine doesn't help then she's going to be in a difficult situation and that it would really help if Jasmine could do it for her. In fact, it is nothing to do with Jasmine that the situation has arisen, and there are solutions that Paula could adopt that wouldn't involve Jasmine (she could rearrange the delivery or decide that on that day her daughter will have to stay at home rather than go to the drama group, or she could ask her husband or another friend to help). By consciously focusing on simply and honestly explaining her own position without over justifying it and without getting too involved in a discussion, Jasmine successfully manages to communicate her 'no' and does so in a polite way. To save herself saying something she regrets she allows herself the extra bit of time to reflect and after the period of reflection she again communicates her message to Paula clearly.

2. Offering a compromise solution

In the key points to remember in saying 'no' to someone you know well, we learned that it may be worth considering a compromise if you are in a situation where you are not very keen on carrying out the request, but would be willing to do so if it is modified or if the other person does something in return for you.

Potential benefits of offering a compromise

The possible benefits from offering a compromise are that:

- If it is agreed, then you and the person you are compromising with may both have an acceptable practical solution instead of a disagreement or stand-off

- It can show that you (and the other person) are reasonable and flexible rather than dogmatic

- It can provide a creative and useful way of working round problems that at first sight appear intractable

- In any long-term or close relationship it is normal to have disagreements sometimes. If you are able to develop the type of relationship where you work together on finding solutions that are acceptable or beneficial to both of you then this can help you to develop trust and goodwill as well as bringing practical benefits.

Possible drawbacks of offering a compromise

In the key points to remember in saying 'no' to someone you know well, we learned that it may be worth considering a compromise *if appropriate*. It is important to remember that it is not always appropriate to offer a compromise. Some drawbacks that can arise from offering a compromise are:

- If the compromise you are offering or agreeing to is not actually a genuine compromise but is really an example of 'giving in' or acceding to a request, then you are sending out a message to the other person that you will not stand up for yourself in a reasonable way. For a compromise to be genuine, you need to get something out of it as well as give something to the other person

- Even if the compromise is genuine, it may still be something which actually goes too far. Before you agree to a compromise it is worth reflecting in your own mind what your 'bottom-line' is, i.e. the point at which for personal, practical or other reasons you are not willing to concede further. Try to stick to that bottom-line, save in exceptional or unpredictable situations

- Sometimes you can lose your self-respect by compromising, and gain nothing. If that is the case then it is better not to compromise. If you feel that the proposed compromise would fundamentally demean you and you are simply compromising to keep harmony, then it may be better not to compromise or to seek advice from an independent person whose judgement you trust.

In many situations, the sensible approach is to reflect on whether a compromise is appropriate for you in that particular situation. This is a matter for individual choice depending on what the situation is and your personal priorities in it. For example, in the case study above, where Jasmine decided on reflection still to say 'no' to Paula, she might instead have decided to offer a compromise. In that case the second phone call could have ended in a different way.

CASE STUDY

Paula and Jasmine: Alternative ending, offering a compromise

Having reflected on the initial phone conversation, Jasmine reflects on the situation and comes up with an alternative that wouldn't be too inconvenient for her but could still help out Paula. She calls Paula back and explains briefly:

Jasmine: 'Hi Paula, I've had a further think about Saturday morning. I do need to get on with my German homework then as I really haven't got much time over the rest of the weekend, but I wonder if there might be an alternative solution. Could you give the delivery people *my* contact phone number and ask them to contact me when they arrive at your house? If you give me a spare key, I can let them into your house when they arrive even if you're out collecting Philippa at the time. That will only take me a few minutes, so I should be able to do my homework too.'

Paula: 'That's a good idea. Thanks. I'll ring the delivery people to let them know. Speak to you later.'

Types of compromise

The kind of compromise offered in the example above is one where the person of whom the request is being made (Jasmine) has found a solution that is not problematic for her. Another type of compromise might be one where

71

Jasmine offers to do the requested task for Paula in return for Paula doing something else for her to help her out (e.g. babysitting later in the week when she needs to go out).

After reading through the preceding sections on 'Saying "no"' and 'Offering a compromise', select (1) one situation where you know you are likely to be asked to do something you don't want to do, and you have decided to say 'no' and *not* offer a compromise, and (2) another situation where you are prepared to offer a compromise in response to a likely request. Try out your selected approach for each situation and compare the results.

---

3. Broken record

The next four assertiveness techniques are considered by Manuel Smith in his book *When I Say No, I Feel Guilty*. The first one is called 'broken record' (or, alternatively, 'scratched record').

The name for this technique comes from the days when musical recordings were commonly played on vinyl records. If a record got scratched you would find that the same phrase of a song or piece of music got repeated over and over again. The broken record technique in relation to assertiveness involves reasserting your request or point repeatedly despite attempts from another person to deflect you or to get you to change it.

The usefulness of the technique is that it gets across to the other person the fact that you are serious in what you are saying and will not be easily fobbed off.

If you are not naturally very assertive you may find your tendency is towards adding unnecessary words, comments or explanations into your assertions. That can deflect from the impact and clarity of what you are saying. The broken record technique helps you instead to focus on the simple message that you want to get across to the other person.

When using the technique it is important to **stay calm in the way that you repeat your point**. This helps to show that you are not being aggressive but simply firm and clear.

Trudy: Using the 'broken record' technique

Trudy purchases her car insurance online. During the purchase process she is asked to input details of any claims she has made in the previous years.

She inputs the relevant details in relation to a previous car accident she had three years before when she was partially at fault and had to make a claim on her policy. The insurance website accepts the details and the quoted premium increases. She purchases the insurance from the website on the basis of that increased quote but when she receives her insurance documents by email she notices that they incorrectly state that she has not made any previous claims. The policy also states that any future claims could be invalidated if she has not supplied correct information.

Trudy telephones the insurance company to get them to correct the policy documentation. After the company has taken the details of the policy number and her name, she explains the situation.

Trudy: 'When I purchased the policy I inputted details of a previous claim I had three years ago and paid an increased premium on the basis of that, but the policy documentation does not record details of the previous claim. Please can you correct the documentation?'

Company representative: 'Are you sure you put the right details in? The website software is set up to record the information submitted. Perhaps you didn't input it correctly?'

Trudy: 'I inputted details of the previous claim. Please can you now correct the documentation.' *[calmly but firmly repeating]*

Company representative: 'The system is automatic – you may not have pressed the right button.'

Trudy: 'The system accepted the information and it produced an increased premium which I paid. Please can you now correct the documentation to record the information I supplied, namely, that I had a previous claim three years ago.' *[calmly repeating her point without getting agitated]*

Company representative: 'We can amend the documentation but there will be an administrative charge for the amendment.'

Trudy: 'I inputted the details before purchasing so there can be no question of an increased charge. Please amend the documentation accordingly.' *[repeating calmly again]*

Company representative: 'I don't have authority to process the amendment without a charge. I suggest you pay the increased charge and then ring back later to see if you can get it refunded.'

Trudy: 'There can be no question of an increased charge and I am not going to ring back later as the fault was yours. Please amend the documentation now.' *[continuing calmly to assert her point]*

Company representative: 'I don't have authority to make the amendment without a charge. If you make the payment of the charge now, I'll make the amendment then pass you on to my manager who can discuss a possible refund with you.'

Trudy (still calm): 'I am not going to pay a charge. I'll wait while you speak to your manager and get authorization to make the amendment.'

Company representative: 'You may have to wait two minutes before I can get through to my manager. Would you like to call back later?'

Trudy (still calm): 'No. I'll wait while you get authorization to make the amendment. Please do so now, explaining that the policy document is incorrect and needs to be corrected.'

Company representative: 'Um, OK – wait a moment'

(After a short silence the Company Representative comes back to the phone.)

Company representative: 'OK that's done – is there anything else I can help you with?'

Trudy: 'No that's fine – just to check: you have now adjusted the policy and it records the previous claim?' *[repeating and checking]*

Company representative: 'Yes.'

Trudy: 'Good – when will I receive confirmation?'

Company representative: 'You will be sent an email within the next 24 hours with the adjusted policy attached or you can log into your account to see it online.'

Trudy: 'OK, thank you.'

(End of conversation.)

When to use the broken record technique

The broken record technique is probably most useful if you are in a formal or commercial situation, such as in the above case study, and you want to make it clear to the other person in a polite way that:

- You are serious about what you are seeking or asserting

- You are not going to be deflected or put off by attempts to change the subject or give a different response or interpretation of the situation

- The request you are making is reasonable.

When to be wary of using the broken record technique

The broken record technique is less likely to be helpful where:

- The request you are making is *unreasonable* or goes significantly beyond your legal rights. For example, in the above case study, if Trudy had in fact forgotten to input the details of the previous accident when buying her insurance and then subsequently requested that her policy details be corrected for free, the company representative might well continue to insist that she pay an administrative charge and might also reasonably ask for an increased premium as the basis of the insurance had changed

- The person you are making the request to is in a *position of bargaining power or authority* in relation to you and has no wish to meet your request. For example, if the police have cordoned off a section of the road and you want to go through the cordon, repeatedly asking the police officer to let you through without a very good reason is highly unlikely to meet with a positive response, because the police officer has the authority and power to refuse your request and no reason to accede to it.

4. Fogging

Fogging is a way of responding to criticism. It involves acknowledging any parts of the criticism which are true, while not responding to other aspects of the criticism or to exaggerations in the criticism. The idea is that your critic, who may be expecting a denial or a riposte which they can then challenge, is instead met by something which it is harder directly to attack (just as if you throw a stone at a fog, it may simply disappear). You acknowledge the literal or partial truth in what the other person is saying, but you don't react to implicit suggestions in what the other person is saying and you don't commit yourself to doing things that the other person may want you to do but hasn't explicitly asked you to do.

Ian and Becky: Using the 'fogging' technique
Becky responds to Ian's criticism of her untidiness by using fogging as follows:

Ian: 'The bedroom is a complete mess!'

Becky: 'You're right – it is messy.' [*Becky is using fogging here, by accepting the element of messiness and not getting involved with responding to the word 'complete' and its implicit negative connotations*]

Ian: 'It really annoys me when you leave the place in such a state.'

Becky: 'Yes, it's true – tidiness isn't one of my strong points.' [*Becky is using fogging here by acknowledging the truth in Ian's statement, without responding to the implied negative comment and value judgement on her]*

Ian: 'Not one of your strong points! You'd make a five-year-old look like the most organized person in the world!'

Becky: 'I agree I'm often not very organized.' *[again, Becky agrees with what she accepts and ignores the pejorative, personal element in Ian's criticism]*

Ian: 'It's maddening – can't you see that it annoys people?'

Becky: 'You're probably right – some people might find it annoying.' *[accepts the statement to a degree without endorsing it wholeheartedly]*

Ian: 'The clothes are all over the place, the wastepaper basket is overflowing and the bed looks like it hasn't been made for a week!'

Becky: 'It's true I didn't make the bed this morning' *[calmly acknowledges an element of truth in Ian's comments without responding to the exaggerations or seeking to justify herself]*

Ian: 'I don't know if you're ever going to change – it's infuriating!'

Becky: "Yes, I can see you're angry about it.' *[acknowledges Ian's sentiment in a calm way but doesn't commit to doing anything in particular]*

When is fogging useful?

Fogging is mainly useful in dealing with *manipulative criticism*. Criticism might be described as manipulative when it is aimed at getting you to do something differently but involves implied moralistic disapproval rather than a straightforward practical request. Faced with this kind of moral disapproval, you may feel an instinct to react defensively or aggressively and feel anxious, guilty or angry. Instead, fogging encourages you to acknowledge those parts of the criticism that may be accurate without allowing yourself to be provoked into an argument.

In this situation fogging can:

- Help you to acknowledge your own tendencies or actions without feeling insecure

- Help you to avoid getting drawn into a slanging match with the other person

- Help you to avoid being manipulated into doing what you don't want to do

- Help you to avoid feelings of anxiety, guilt or anger.

When is fogging not helpful?
Fogging is not usually helpful if the other person thinks that you are being sarcastic or patronizing in your responses, as this may simply lead them to become wound up or aggressive. For that reason bear in mind the tips below.

 Key elements to remember if you are using the fogging technique are:

- Don't react defensively

- Stay calm and receptive

- Don't respond by denial or criticisms of your own

- Don't be sarcastic in your tone (this is likely to provoke an aggressive or critical response from the other person).

All of these key elements also apply to the next two assertion techniques: negative assertion and negative inquiry.

5. Negative assertion

Negative assertion means acknowledging mistakes that you have made or actions that you have committed that with hindsight you regret, or other features that you would prefer to be different about you. It involves honestly admitting to mistakes, failings or misjudgements.

Many of us react defensively when someone criticizes us or some aspect of our appearance or behaviour. Perhaps the reason for this is that we feel that if we admit to a mistake or to having done something 'wrong' or performed less well than we would like, then this means that we are a 'failure' or 'bad'. Actually, admitting to faults or failings is often a positive thing to do as your critic may then feel disarmed and appreciate your acknowledgement. You may also have a platform from which to make positive changes if you want to, without feeling guilty.

CASE STUDY

Tom and Annette: Using the 'negative assertion' technique

Tom has gone to the barber and come back with a haircut which doesn't look great. When Annette points this out to him he is about to react defensively but then calmly agrees.

Annette: Oh dear, that haircut, didn't quite work out for you, did it?

Tom: [about to react defensively then decides to use negative assertion] 'You're right. I probably shouldn't go to that place again!'

Annette: 'They didn't even trim your eyebrows either!'

Tom: 'True, that would probably look better. Next time I'll try a different barber.'

As you can see from the above discussion, negative assertion is not so much about dealing with moralistic manipulative criticism (which is the main use of fogging). It is more about being open in acknowledging your personal mistakes or faults in the face of critical comments which are true. Remember, it is OK to make mistakes!

How is negative assertion useful?

If you act defensively when people offer truthful criticism of you, then through your defensiveness or denial you may fuel further prolonged criticism from the other person or prompt another unhelpful reaction from them. You yourself may start to feel guilty or bad about how you have acted, so simply acknowledging the truth and holding your hands up to having done something you regret is often sensible. It can take the sting out of the criticism and lead to a more constructive relationship going forward.

When negative assertion can be unhelpful

If admitting your mistake or error may have significant legal implications then it may be sensible not to use negative assertion. Manuel Smith gives the example of a car accident and suggests that it is not necessarily wise to admit to fault at the scene of the accident but instead to exchange insurance details. The technique is intended for use in social dealings, not in potential legal conflicts!

6. Negative inquiry

With negative assertion you acknowledge mistakes or faults. With negative inquiry you take this a step further and actively *invite* further or encourage further or more detailed criticism.

Chloe and James: Using the 'negative inquiry' technique

Chloe and James are eating their evening meal together and James makes a comment about the way Chloe eats.

James (in an irritated, disgusted voice): 'Stop eating like that!'

Chloe (speaking calmly and curiously): 'I'm not sure I understand. What is it about the way I eat that creates a problem?' *[Chloe invites clarification of the negative comment]*

James: 'It's the way you chomp at the food.'

Chloe (still calm and curious): 'Oh – is it the noise I make or my mouth being open when I eat or something else?'

James: 'It's both of those things!'

Chloe (still calm): 'I see – the sound and the look of it aren't very nice. Might that create problems for us?' *[Chloe invites further negative comment, showing herself open to and accepting of criticism]*

James: 'Our friends may think you haven't got any manners.'

Chloe (still calm): 'You mean I'm acting in a way that might make us lose friends?'

James (backing down a bit but then resuming his irritation): 'Not necessarily but it could be embarrassing for us. I don't know which way to look sometimes when you're eating.'

Chloe (still calm and curious): 'I'm not sure I fully understand – how would it be embarrassing for us?'

James: 'Well, I would feel embarrassed by it, that's all – I would prefer it if you didn't do it.'

Chloe: *[reflecting and inviting further negative comment]* 'I see – I'll think about it and see what I can do. Are there any other habits I have which cause a problem?'

James: 'Well, you do hold your knife and fork in rather a clumsy way.'

Chloe: Can you show me?'

(James then demonstrates how Chloe holds her knife and fork.)

Chloe (calm and curious still): 'I see – that way of holding a knife and fork might be seen as clumsy – and that could create similar potentially embarrassing situations could it?'

James (calm now): 'Yes – I would feel embarrassed by it. I would prefer it if you did it this way.'

(He demonstrates how he would like Chloe to hold the knife and fork).

In the above example, Chloe has used negative inquiry by calmly seeking further clarification about what aspects of her behaviour are seen by James as potentially problematic and why. This shows that she can handle the criticism and it takes the heat out of the situation, giving James no reason to get further agitated. It is important to note that in her inquiries, Chloe does not criticize James's views or suggest that it is a matter of his personal taste or preference. For example, she doesn't say, 'What is your problem with the way I eat?', which might imply that the issue is about his personal preference and would potentially focus attention on him rather than on her behaviour.

It is perhaps precisely because Chloe uses the neutral, inquiring and puzzled questions rather than suggesting it is a matter of James's personal preference, that the end result is that he himself acknowledges that it is a matter of his own personal preference and feelings. He then explains clearly what he would like, rather than haranguing her in an irritated and judgemental way.

How is negative inquiry useful?

Negative inquiry encourages the person who is being critical of you to be assertive rather than derogatory in their requests, which is likely to lead to a healthier form of communication. The technique helps to clarify what it is that the other person wants you to do and why. In the above example, the use of negative inquiry by Chloe prompts James to express in a clearer and more polite way that he would like Chloe to eat more quietly and to hold her knife and fork differently, because he feels embarrassed in the presence of others when she is eating like that. Now that he has expressed what he wants in this clearer way, it is open to Chloe to decide whether to do what he requests or alternatively to explain to him that she doesn't want to do so or else to ask for something in return from him. In other words, negative inquiry has helped to create the possibility of a healthier, more practical dialogue.

When to use negative inquiry

Manuel Smith suggested that the negative inquiry technique works best in unstructured equal relationships, such as in conversations with people you are close to rather than in formal relationships. Potential benefits of using negative inquiry in this kind of situation are that it can:

- Help you to listen to legitimate criticisms from people close to you rather than to dismiss or deny them

- Stop repetitive, manipulative criticism from those people towards you, since they are likely to respond differently to your negative inquiry than they would do to defensiveness or denial

- Prompt those people to express their personal wishes and preferences more clearly (assertively) rather than to speak in a moralistic way, imposing their own views of right and wrong without owning them as such.

The best way to find out if negative inquiry works in this way for you is to try the technique out, but remember not to be sarcastic if you do so – try to use a tone of genuine inquiry.

 Once you have familiarized yourself with what is involved in the broken record technique, fogging, negative assertion and negative inquiry then try out one or more of the techniques and assess the results.

7. DESC scripting

DESC scripting is a method for encouraging people to change behaviour that is unpleasant, unreasonable or unacceptable to you. It involves informing them of how you will react if they don't' change their behaviour and then carrying through on that commitment if they don't change their behaviour. DESC stands for:

Describe: say what the behaviour is that you don't find acceptable

Express: explain briefly your thoughts and feelings about it

Specify: state what you would like them to do about it

Consequences: say what the consequences will be if they don't do this (or you can specify positive consequences that will occur if they do change their behaviour!)

 Negative consequences that you decide to apply if someone doesn't change their behaviour should be reasonable and proportionate in the circumstances.

 Tina and Mark: Using the DESC scripting technique
Tina's husband Mark has developed a severe alcohol problem. He is refusing to seek

professional support for it and has not been able to do anything about it through his own efforts. Tina realizes that it is not sensible or helpful for her or the children simply to put up with the problems that this is causing the family. She uses the **DESC** acronym to help her prepare a script for what she will say to Mark.

> **D**escribe: 'I know that you have been trying to deal with your alcohol problem on your own, but unfortunately you haven't managed to get control of it.'

> **E**xpress: 'I think that you need to get professional support to help you with it. I am also worried that if you don't do so, the children will suffer because they keep seeing you drunk, shouting, getting annoyed and not taking care of yourself.'

> **S**pecify: 'I would like you to go to see our doctor or an alcohol support agency.'

> **C**onsequences: 'I have decided that if you don't do so within the next week then I am going to move out to my sister's with the children.'

Tina puts together the statements she has written down using the DESC acronym into a script which she learns. When there is a reasonable opportunity to put across her view and decision to Mark (when the children are in bed), she informs him of what she has decided:

'There is something that I need to discuss with you. I know that you have been trying to deal with your alcohol problem on your own, but unfortunately you haven't managed to get control of it. I think that you need to get professional support to help you with it. I am also worried that if you don't do so, the children will suffer because they keep seeing you drunk, shouting, getting annoyed and not taking care of yourself. I would like you to go to see our doctor or an alcohol support agency. I have decided that if you don't so within the next week then I am going to move out to my sister's with the children.'

The above example involves a situation where it is probably important to stress *negative* consequences that will ensue if Mark *doesn't* seek support – not least because the welfare of their children is involved. In some circumstances however, when you want someone to act in a particular way, it can be more productive to stress *positive* consequences that will ensue if the other person *does* act in the way that you want, rather than negative consequences that will ensue if they don't change their behaviour. This can act as an incentive and sound like less of a criticism. 'If you free up some time for the weekend, I'll cook you your favourite dinner' may sometimes be a more successful approach than 'If you don't free up some time for the weekend, I won't cook your dinner'!

When you know that you are in a situation where you need to enforce boundaries in a relationship or to show someone that there will be consequences if they continue to act in a certain way, try using a DESC script to help you deal with the situation. Remember, only specify consequences that you are prepared to carry out. Ideally, the other person will adapt their behaviour before you need to carry out negative consequences that you think are reasonable and have informed them of, but if they don't adapt their behaviour, hold the courage of your convictions and do what you said you would do unless there is a very strong reason not to do so.

Key ideas from chapter 3

Some of the key ideas in chapter 3 are:

- In saying 'no', be clear and explicit and keep your explanations simple if possible

- Offering a compromise solution (p. 68) is sometimes sensible but it may be helpful to weigh up the possible advantages and disadvantages first

- In formal or commercial situations the 'broken record' technique (p. 72) can help you to avoid being put off or diverted from what you are saying

- Fogging (p. 78) can be a useful approach for dealing with manipulative criticism, but beware of being sarcastic or patronizing

- Negative assertion and negative inquiry (pp. 81–87) can help to disarm your critics and create a constructive environment for dialogue

- You can use the DESC scripting technique (p. 88) to help encourage others to change behaviour that is creating problems for you.

We have now finished section 1 of the book relating to assertiveness basics and are ready to move on to section 2, relating to ways of changing different kinds of non-assertive behaviour that you might have a tendency towards. In the first part of section 2, you will find techniques for changing passive behaviour.

SECTION 2: CHANGING NON-ASSERTIVE BEHAVIOUR

4. Changing passive behaviour – gaining the courage to assert yourself

In the introduction to this book, we looked at two kinds of behaviour that are not assertive: passive behaviour and aggressive behaviour. In this chapter, we will explore ideas for dealing with tendencies towards passive behaviour, and in the following chapter we will look into ways of dealing with tendencies towards aggressive behaviour.

Passive behaviour

Passive behaviour is behaviour that is characteristic of people who seek to avoid conflict or criticism – you try too much to please others at your own expense and often avoid expressing your own views or feelings in situations where a more assertive person might do so. In the introduction, five characteristics that might indicate a tendency to passive behaviour were highlighted:

1. Going along with other people's decisions even if you don't agree with them because you don't want to have an argument.

2. Taking on an excessive share of unpleasant or mundane tasks because you feel that it would be confrontational to say 'no' or you are worried about the consequences of saying 'no'.

3. Agreeing to do things you don't want to do because you are overly concerned with trying to please people or don't want to upset them.

4. Failing to express or communicate your true feelings (particularly when these involve contradicting another person or criticizing them) because of anxieties about the effect on your relationship or worries that people may then have a negative opinion of you.

5. Being unaware of your rights or afraid to exercise them, or believing that you should always be deferential or compliant towards others.

 Read through the above characteristics of passive behaviour. Which ones do you think apply to you? Using the headings below, note down details of situations where you have a tendency to act passively.

(a) Type of situation (e.g. work, home, social relationships, romantic relationships, dealing with people in authority).

(b) Who do you tend to act passively towards? (Make a note of any particular individuals with whom you are more passive.)

(c) Ways in which your behaviour is passive. (Which of the five characteristics highlighted above are relevant?)

When trying out suggested methods and exercises later on in this chapter, look back at the details in your notes and apply the techniques to the situations you have highlighted.

Using the ABC model to change passive thinking

If you have a tendency to behave passively and not stand up for yourself or express your thoughts and feelings, the likelihood is that you are placing an anxious interpretation on the situation or worrying about what might happen if you assert yourself. One approach that you can use to address anxious thoughts is the ABC model devised by the psychologist Albert Ellis for analysing links between thoughts, feelings and actions. This can be used to great effect to address passive thinking patterns which may be underlying your passive actions. The ABC model encourages you to analyse an event and your response in terms of **A**, the activating event, **B**, your belief about its significance and **C**, your consequent emotions and behaviour. Below is a case study showing how the model can be used in an instance where someone behaves passively because of their anxious interpretation of the situation.

Julian: ABC model analysis of passive behaviour

Julian emails his friend, Sarah, to suggest meeting up. She doesn't respond. He starts to worry about why she hasn't responded, and consequently dithers. Here is an analysis of the situation using the ABC model.

Activating event
Julian emails Sarah, to suggest they meet in the evening. The evening comes and she has not responded.

↓

Belief
'She is usually reliable. I must have offended her so she's ignored my email.'

↓

Consequences
Emotions: Julian feels anxious.
Behaviour: Julian slips into his habitual *passive* form of behaviour, deciding not to do anything, because he is worrying about what Sarah's response might be and doesn't want a confrontation or embarrassing situation.

Challenging passive thinking

If you find yourself behaving passively because of anxious thoughts and you want to behave more assertively, it is usually helpful to *challenge* those anxious thoughts so that the block to asserting yourself is lessened or put into perspective. The idea is to make your thought patterns more *realistic*.

Here is a **challenge checklist** of seven questions that you can run through when your anxious thoughts inhibit your actions, in order to adapt your mindset and help you to think and act in a sensible assertive way. You can go through all of the questions or just select those that you consider most helpful for you.

1. What evidence is there to support my anxious belief? What evidence is there to cast doubt on it?

2. What alternative possibilities are there and what evidence is there to suggest they might be true? Which possibility is most likely?

3. Is the anxious belief helpful? What problems are caused by me believing it?

4. If my belief is true, how much does it matter?

5. What could I do to find out if my belief is true?

6. If my belief is true, what is the most constructive way I could react?

7. What might a more accurate or moderate belief or interpretation be?

When challenging your anxious thoughts, the idea is not to dismiss them out of hand, it is to put them into perspective and to evaluate them in a reasonable and practical way. If there is some truth in your beliefs, you can acknowledge that but recognize where you are exaggerating or being inflexible and moderate your view accordingly. This way, the grip of the anxious thought is lessened.

 If you still find it difficult to put your anxious thoughts in perspective, one further thing you can try is to ask yourself what you would say to a friend who described a situation like the one you are in and expressed a similar belief about what it meant. This may prompt you to come up with a more balanced, less anxious viewpoint.

 Julian (continued): Using a challenge checklist to address anxiety
Julian uses the questions on the challenge checklist to analyse his anxious belief that he may have offended his friend and comes up with the following answers.

1. What evidence is there to support my belief? What evidence is there to cast doubt on it?

In support of my belief: 'I haven't received a response from Sarah to my email invitation which is unusual because she is normally reliable.'

Against my belief: 'I can't think of anything I've done that might have caused offence and Sarah doesn't normally react by ignoring me if we have a disagreement.'

2. What alternative possibilities are there and what evidence is there to suggest they might be true? Which is most likely?

There are several other possibilities, including:

- The email may not have got through or she may not have opened it yet

- Perhaps she is not in her office for some reason today so has not seen the email

- She might have meant to respond but got distracted by something else and forgotten

- She might have responded and the email hasn't got through to me

- She might have been unable to go or been very busy, and thought that if she did not respond I would realize she could not meet me

- She might have had to deal with something that for her was very important, and not got round to answering the email

- There might be another explanation I haven't thought of – things quite often happen which I haven't envisaged. I know I have a tendency to expect the worst and often reality isn't so dire.

'Any of these possibilities could be true. I can't really estimate what is most likely until I make further enquiries.'

3. *Is the belief helpful? What problems are caused by me believing it?*
'The belief isn't very helpful because it causes me anxiety and I have reacted by putting off contacting Sarah again because of my worry.'

4. *If my belief is true, how much does it matter?*
'It matters in that I don't want to cause offence to Sarah, but it's not the end of the world. If I ring her there's a good chance we can sort it out.'

5. *What could I do to check out if my belief is true?*
'I could call Sarah or ask her when I next speak to her.'

6. *If my belief is true, what is the most constructive way I could react?*
'Try to find out what upset her and apologize if appropriate.'

7. What might a more accurate or moderate belief be?
'I could reframe the belief in a more moderate and accurate way: "It is possible that Sarah thinks I have offended her but there are other possibilities and it is unlike her to react in that kind of way. Even if it's true there's no point in worrying about it – I'll ring her tomorrow to check it out if she hasn't contacted me by then. If I have offended her then I'll apologize if it turns out I've been insensitive in some way."'

Julian reminds himself of this more moderate belief and uses it to motivate himself to ring Sarah the next day. It turns out that her elderly mother had a fall shortly before he emailed. Sarah was preoccupied by that and forgot to respond to his email. She apologizes to him and they arrange to meet later in the week.

 A **balancing thought** (which can also be called a 'balancing statement') is a statement that you say to yourself to help you put into perspective negative, anxious or self-critical thoughts. The more accurate or moderate belief that you come up with in response to question 7 on the challenge checklist is a balancing thought that you can remind yourself of to help you act differently, just as Julian does in the above case study.

Think of a situation you have been involved in where you acted passively due to anxious beliefs. Analyse the situation using the ABC model and then answer the questions in the challenge checklist to arrive at a balancing thought for your anxious beliefs. Remind yourself of it the next time you are in a similar situation and use it as an aid to acting more assertively where that is sensible.

If you find that there are particular questions on the challenge checklist that are more helpful for you than others, then you can focus your attention on those questions rather than going through all seven questions each time.

Facing up to your fears of being assertive

Catastrophizing (also known as 'awfulizing')
Sometimes people fail to express themselves or hesitate to object or request a change in the way someone else is acting towards them, because of *fear* of the consequences. When this tendency to imagine the worst becomes a mental habit, it is called *catastrophizing* or *awfulizing* – an exaggerated belief that negative consequences will ensue or that they will be much worse or harder to bear than the evidence actually suggests.

To deal with any catastrophizing tendencies, it is usually helpful to draw them out into the open and analyse them in a practical way. Here is a suggested five-step process for doing so.

Step 1: Consider options

Draw up a list of the options available to you for how you might act in the situation you are in and to highlight for each option the advantages and disadvantages of trying out that option. Usually, the first option will be to continue behaving as you have been and not change your normal way of acting. Start off by writing that down and identifying the advantages and disadvantages of that, then think of some alternative options for how you could act and write down the advantages and disadvantages of each of them. At this stage you are not committing yourself to anything, you are just examining the different possibilities in a reasonably objective way.

Step 2: Select the assertive option

Once you have written down your list of options and their advantages and disadvantages, ask yourself which option you would choose if you were the kind of 'assertive' person you want to be, bearing in mind that an assertive person is someone who:

- Expresses their views clearly and articulately without being aggressive

- Stands up for their own and other people's rights in a reasonable and clear way

- Allows other people a reasonable opportunity to express their opinions without allowing them to dominate a conversation.

Step 3: Face your fears

Once you have selected your 'assertive' option, face up to what fears you have about following that 'assertive' option by answering the following set of questions:

(i) What is the worst that could happen if I act assertively?

(ii) How likely as a percentage is it to happen?

(iii) Is there anything I can do to reduce that percentage?

(iv) If it does happen will it still be worth me having acted assertively?

(v) What can I do to deal with it if it does happen?

Step 4: Decide how you are going to act

Having faced up to your fears about being assertive, decide if you think it is worth trying to be assertive in this situation. If you are in doubt, then reflect again on the advantages and disadvantages of the different options you set out in step 1. You do not have to choose the assertive option, but quite often your objective analysis may lead you to conclude that it is worth trying out and that your fears about acting assertively were exaggerated or unrealistic. If you do decide that objectively it is worth trying to be assertive, but you still hesitate because you are out of your comfort zone, then you can help to reinforce your commitment to act assertively by answering the following questions.

(i) What will help to ensure that I carry out the action? Some things you might consider could be:

- setting a specific occasion or time to do the action

- carrying a list with you of the benefits of doing the action that you can refer to

- writing a preparatory script of what you might say (if the option is going to involve you in speaking).

(ii) Will it help me to get support from someone else (e.g. by explaining what I am going to do to a trusted friend) or may this hinder me?

(iii) Do I want to take the course of action all in one go, or do I want to try to break it down into steps or smaller actions in some way?

Step 5: Act
Once you have made your decision as to how you are going to act, then carry out your commitment and proceed to act. After doing so, reflect on the outcome. If it has been

positive, then try to act in a similar way if a similar situation arises again. If for some reason the action hasn't turned out as successfully as you would like, then still give yourself credit for trying it out and reflect on whether there is anything you might do differently next time in a similar situation, so that you can learn from the experience.

Sangita: Facing up to your fears of being assertive

Sangita has a close but sometimes difficult relationship with her mother who is frequently critical of her. Last week Sangita ended her relationship with her boyfriend, which hadn't been working out. When she told her mother, her mother responded by suggesting that her boyfriend had been the best thing that ever happened to her and saying 'How could you ruin that relationship like all the others?' Sangita felt hurt and angry but from long ago her tendency when communicating with her mother has been to behave passively for fear of creating confrontation and argument, so when her mother levelled this accusation at her initially she did not respond despite her feelings. Sangita uses the five-step process for facing up to her fears of being assertive when communicating with her mother.

Step 1: Consider options

Sangita draws up a list of possible courses of action she could take in the way that she responds to her mother's repeated criticism, starting with the option of doing nothing. She lists the advantages and disadvantages of each option, trying to be as objective as she can.

Option 1: Do nothing and continue to relate to my mother in the way I have always done

Advantages	Disadvantages
• I have been in this situation before. I don't like it, but at least I am not taking unknown risks which I am worried might make things even worse	• I will continue to feel angry and upset inside • My mother's behaviour is unlikely to change if I do nothing • I may feel that I am pathetic because I have done nothing

Option 2: Don't overtly challenge my mother but start to distance myself from her, having less contact

Advantages	Disadvantages
• By having less contact with my mother there would be less opportunity for her to put me down	• My mother may react adversely, e.g. by criticizing me for not contacting her • I may feel guilty

Option 3: Raise the issue with my mother and explain to her how I would like her to act differently

Advantages	Disadvantages
• I would be showing that I can be a more proactive positive person • I would be expressing my feelings • My mother might understand me better • My mother might begin to change her behaviour	• My mother might react even more angrily and be even more critical of me • I might feel that I had been unfair to her

Option 4: Ask another family member – my father or sister/ brother to raise the issue with my mother

Advantages	Disadvantages
• My mother might get a better idea of my feelings and might change her behaviour	• I would be relying on someone else to act on my behalf, and would not have control over exactly what they said or whether they put the point across in the way I would like • I would only know about the conversation at second hand, rather than being there and knowing what really happened • My mother might not change her behaviour

Step 2: Select the assertive option

Sangita reflects on the options and decides that if she were more assertive in this situation she would follow option 3 (raising the issue with her mother and explaining how she would like her mother to act differently).

Step 3: Face your fears

Sangita analyses the **worst case** that could happen if she pursues her preferred option.

(i) What is the worst that could happen if I act assertively?
'My mother could get angry and be even more critical. She might not speak to me for a few days.'

(ii) How likely as a percentage is it to happen?
'On the basis of past experience, I think the probability of the worst case scenario arising here is about 50 per cent.'

(iii) Is there anything I can do to reduce that percentage?
'If I don't get angry myself and just make my point simply and calmly and then leave Mum to reflect on it rather than getting drawn into an argument, this would probably reduce the likelihood of my mother reacting in that way to about ten per cent.'

(iv) If it does happen will it still be worth me having acted assertively?

'Even if the worst case scenario does arise it will prob-ably be worth it. I will feel better for having made my point simply and clearly. I would prefer Mum not to choose not to speak to me for a few days but it's her choice. Even if that happens, she will resume talking to me at some point so it wouldn't be the end of the world.'

(v) What can I do to deal with it if it does happen?
'If the worst case scenario does arise and Mum ignores me for a few days, the best thing I can do will be to remind myself that I have a right to be treated with respect and that I have expressed my views in a reason-able, clear way.'

Step 4: Decide how you are going to act

Reflecting on her different options and her analysis of the worst case, Sangita decides that in this situation it *is* worth trying to be assertive. She decides to try to raise the issue with her mother in a calm and clear way, without labouring the point. To reinforce her commitment to act in this asser-tive way, she answers the suggested questions for step 4.

(i) What will help to ensure that I carry out the action?
'I will plan a sensible way of approaching the situation, probably by:

(a) praising my mother for expressing her emotions first

(b) then saying that in some situations however I would prefer it if she was a little less critical of me, and highlighting the example of her criticism of me for ending the relationship

(c) then finishing by saying that I mention it because I would really like for us to stay close and I think that will help.'

(This is an example of an 'assertion sandwich' where the criticism (b) is sandwiched in between two positives (a) and (c) – see p 45.)

(ii) Will it help me to get support from someone else?
'On this occasion I think that this is something I need to do for myself and don't need to seek support on.'

(iii) Do I want to take the course of action all in one go, or do I want to try to break it down into steps or smaller actions in some way?
'In this case it is best to deal with the issue in one go, I think, rather than prolong it.'

Step 5: Act

Sangita tries out her course of action. Her mother's reaction is instinctively defensive and she criticizes Sangita for raising the issue. In accordance with her plan, Sangita doesn't allow herself to get drawn into a discussion about it. On this occasion, over the next week the worst case scenario doesn't arise. In fact, her mother acts in a friendly way towards her and Sangita feels that her actions may have had a positive effect for their relationship, even if her mother is unlikely to acknowledge that explicitly. She is pleased that she took the assertive course of action.

Positive visualization

If you have difficulty in believing that you are going to be able to act assertively or carry out tasks effectively, then you can practise positive visualization to help you prepare for what you want to attempt. In the above case study, Sangita could use the positive visualization exercise below to help prepare herself for talking to her mother. You could also use it for other situations where you feel anxious and want to act more assertively, such as a job interview or a presentation you have to make. You can practise the visualization exercise on a daily basis for a few days to help you build up the association of confidence and relaxation with what you are going to do, before you enter the situation for real.

To do your positive visualization exercise:

1. Find a quiet place where you can practise the visualization free from any distractions

2. Do a relaxation exercise for a few minutes to get you into a relaxed frame of mind. You could try the simple relaxation exercise given below, or you could use your

own if you are familiar with a relaxation technique that works well for you.

Relaxation exercise
Shut your eyes and imagine yourself in a place or environment that you find enjoyable, doing something relaxing and pleasurable. This will vary depending on what you as an individual like. You could, for example, be by a lake or at the sea or in beautiful scenery, or you could imagine yourself socializing with good friends or on a journey. Whatever situation you choose, make sure it is a harmonious one and not connected with current activities or stresses. The exercise should take you into a relaxing world.

Once you are in that relaxing world, try to imagine it in as much detail as you can – what sounds can you hear, what sensations are you experiencing in your body, who or what else is there, what is happening between yourself and others or the environment?

3. After a few minutes of doing the relaxation exercise, when you are fully relaxed, in your mind move in a calm, accepting way from the relaxing imaginary environment into imagining the challenging situation where you want to be assertive, and focus now in a positive, confident way on the task at hand. Use all your senses to help with the visualization: imagine what your surroundings

look like, what sounds there are, any smells or tastes or touch-related sensations.

4. Imagine yourself starting to act effectively, confidently and successfully. If it helps, imagine that you are doing it in the same way that someone you know who is good at doing the task would do it, or focus on a positive role model whom you admire and imagine yourself acting like them.

5. If you start to feel nervous at any point in the process, then calm yourself by focusing on breathing in a slow measured way in and out, counting your breaths. Reassure yourself that it is OK to get nervous, then refocus on the task in a confident way reminding yourself that you can do it.

6. Imagine yourself continuing with and completing the task successfully, and dealing constructively and practically with any problems that arise or difficult reactions from the other person.

7. Imagine any benefits that you get from having completed the task in the way you wanted, including any positive practical outcomes but also your own feelings of achievement at having been assertive, whatever the result.

Once you have finished your positive reflections, open your eyes again slowly, draw yourself back into the present and then resume your normal daily activities.

Think of a situation you are acting passively in because of fear of the consequences of being more assertive. To help you decide what to do in the situation, go through steps 1–4 of the five step process for dealing with catastrophizing tendencies (see p. 103ff). Remember, you do not need to act assertively if, after your analysis, you conclude that for sensible reasons in this case it is preferable to be passive, but if your analysis suggests that your worst fears are unjustified or that you can deal with them if they arise, then in that case consider trying out a more assertive option than you have been doing in the situation. If you decide to try to be more assertive, then if you want you can use the positive visualization exercise to help you prepare to act in that more assertive way by visualizing yourself acting confidently and effectively in your new assertive role.

How to get your point across

The ABC Model and the five step process for dealing with catastrophizing tendencies can help you to deal with anxieties and fears about what might happen if you are assertive. Sometimes it is also useful to have a structure that will guide you in *how to put your point across.* If you are in a situation where you want to request a change or to ask someone to make changes in their behaviour and you are not quite sure how to go about it, you can use a framework called the 'DEAL method'. It is similar to the DESC (Describe – Express

– Specify – Consequences) scripting technique described in chapter 3 (p. 88) but contains some additional elements. In particular, the DESC scripting technique encourages you simply to state consequences if your request is not met, whereas the DEAL method is more flexible, encouraging you to listen and negotiate a solution. It is therefore preferable to use the DEAL method, unless the situation is one where there is no room for dialogue or compromise.

The **DEAL method** is a structured process for seeking a change in a situation you are not happy with, or where another other person is acting in a way that is problematic for you. The acronym 'DEAL' indicates how to go about requesting change(s). DEAL stands for:

Describe the situation or behaviour that is troubling you

Express your thoughts about it

Ask for reasonable changes that you feel would help

Listen and negotiate for a reasonable solution if possible

The DEAL method builds on four key elements of assertive behaviour:

- Clarity
- Reasonableness
- Honesty
- Respect.

In particular, the approach is about *reasonableness*. Remember that it reasonable for you to express your own wishes and needs in a polite but assertive way, and then follow the DEAL method in doing that. Here is an example that shows how you might use the method to discuss a difficult issue in a work situation. You can also use it in many personal situations where you want to express your views on something, and seek a change from someone you know or are in a relationship with.

In using the DEAL method, it is often helpful to run through the steps *before* you raise the issue, and prepare what you are going to say when you raise the issue and how you are going to discuss it.

CASE STUDY

Andrea: Using the DEAL method to request changes

Andrea is in a work situation where her boss Gillian frequently gives her more work than she can cope with. One Monday morning, Andrea arrives at work and unexpectedly finds a file of papers on her desk, together with a scribbled note from Gillian: 'Could you look through these and give me a briefing note ready for Friday. Thanks. Gillian.' Andrea has already got a full schedule for the week, so doing the briefing note is going to present problems. Andrea uses the DEAL acronym to help her decide how to raise the issue with Gillian and to prepare what she will say.

Step 1: Describe the situation to the other person

In describing the situation it usually helps to *be specific and clear*, indicating what the problem is, keeping your statement simple if possible and trying to be accurate in what you say rather than using emotive or generalized language. Andrea rehearses the following simple description of the problem to say to her boss Gillian.

> 'I've had a quick look at the papers that you've asked me to do the briefing note on for Friday. Unfortunately, I've already got a full schedule for this week.'

Step 2: Express your thoughts about the situation

Andrea prepares a simple statement of her thoughts about the situation.

> 'I don't think I'm going to be able to complete the briefing note by Friday unless I drop something else.'

Andrea's statement has the following features:

- It is simple and accurate

- She is using an 'I' statement (as previously recommended for being assertive – see p. 39).

Sometimes, it will be relevant to express your *feelings* as well as your thoughts, if this is something that you feel is important to communicate to the other person. In this situation, if Andrea felt that was important, she might include in the statement a sentence such as: 'I feel frustrated that I've been asked to do something without being asked first whether it is practical for me to do in the allocated time.' This would not be overly emotional language, simply a clear statement of the feelings engendered by the other person's actions.

Step 3: Ask for reasonable changes that you feel would help

It is useful if you can come up with a constructive suggestion indicating what would resolve the problem for you. Andrea decides on a simple request.

'Could I have another few days to complete the briefing note?'

Combining steps 1–3, Andrea has now created a simple, clear description of the situation and her thoughts, ending with an appropriate request. In full, the **DEAL request** that she has prepared goes as follows:

'I've had a quick look at the papers that you've asked me to do the briefing note on for Friday. Unfortunately, I've already got a full schedule for this week. I don't think I'm going to be able to complete the briefing note by Friday unless I drop something else. Could I have another few days to complete it?'

Step 4: Listen and negotiate a reasonable solution where possible

Often, the other person may have a different perspective on the situation to you. If you have not voiced your concerns before or have done so in an unassertive way, they may not even be aware of the concerns until you express them clearly for the first time. Alternatively, they may have their own agendas or pressures that they want to meet, which may conflict with yours.

In Andrea's situation, if Gillian responds to her request by agreeing to move the deadline back a few days then a satisfactory solution will have been reached quickly. However, that might not be practical or Gillian might be keen to get the briefing note quickly for her own reasons. Once you have made your request, you therefore need to be prepared to listen to what the other person says and, if required, to negotiate a reasonable solution if your first request is not immediately agreed to.

To prepare yourself for negotiating around your request, read through the negotiation tips in chapter 2 (p. 53) and decide on any negotiating points that are important to you. Having read through those tips, Andrea makes a note to do the following.

- She decides that if Gillian says that she cannot move the deadline, then she will explain that she won't be able to do all her other scheduled tasks, and she will ask Gillian to advise her as to which of her currently scheduled tasks she can drop out of in order to make time to do the briefing note. (This is an example of using negotiation tips 5 and 6 (pp. 53–54), thinking about how to move the discussion forward and offering a compromise)

- She decides that she is not prepared to work outside her normal working hours to complete the task (negotiation tip 2 (p. 52) – identifying what you are not willing to compromise on) and that if Gillian insists she does the briefing note as well as all her other tasks, then she will explain that this is likely to mean that some of the tasks will not get done as well as they should be, as she won't have sufficient time to check them all thoroughly

- She decides that she will keep a written note of whatever is agreed (negotiation tip 14, p. 56) and of any points of disagreement. If problems arise subsequently from her being given an excessive workload or from Gillian not remembering (or choosing not to remember) the discussion, or from Gillian ignoring Andrea's request, then Andrea will have a reference note which will help to show that she highlighted the problems for her workload in an appropriate way and what the outcome was.

After preparing her **DEAL statement**, Andrea makes her request. In this case, the outcome is as follows: Gillian is not prepared to move the deadline for the briefing note, but she *does* agree that Andrea can give her apologies to a meeting she had been scheduled to attend, as it is not a priority, and Andrea is able to use that time to prepare the briefing note.

 Complete the exercise below to help you prepare to highlight a situation where you would like to see a change.

Using the DEAL method to prepare to be assertive
Step 1: Describe the situation
Follow the principles described above to formulate one or two sentences that you might use when describing the situation you are concerned about. Keep your description as short and clear as you can and express it in the first person (i.e. beginning 'I').

Step 2: Express your thoughts about the situation
Now follow the principles described above to formulate one or two sentences that you might use to communicate your thoughts on the situation and your feelings if appropriate.

Step 3: Ask for reasonable changes that you feel would help
Next, set out in one to two sentences the request that you would like to make or a possible proposal that you feel would improve the situation.

Put together Steps 1–3 to create a DEAL request that you can say to the other person.

Step 4: Listen and negotiate a reasonable solution where possible
Read through the negotiation tips (p. 53) to highlight relevant points for you in trying to reach a compromise or a solution. Make a note of any particularly relevant tips in your situation and how you can apply them.

Key ideas from chapter 4
Key ideas to remember in particular from chapter 4 are:

- Passive behaviour is characteristic of people who want to avoid conflict or criticism

- Passive behaviour often follows from anxiety about what will happen if you assert yourself

- You can use a challenge checklist (p. 97) to assess how realistic your anxious thoughts are

- If you have a tendency to catastrophize (imagine the worst) about the possible results of acting assertively, then try the five-step process for facing your fears (p. 103)

- Positive visualization (p. 112) can help you to prepare for attempting to act more assertively

- Use the DEAL method (p. 116) to get your point across in a situation where you want to request a change in behaviour from someone.

---

5. Changing aggressive behaviour – learning to act reasonably

The other side of the coin from passive behaviour is aggressive behaviour. Much of the literature around becoming assertive focuses on standing up for yourself and resisting unreasonable demands, if your tendency is to let other people take advantage of your goodwill or persuade you to do things that you do not really want or need to do. But what if your tendency is the opposite? If, far from being too passive in some situations, you actually have a tendency to be too aggressive or too demanding, what can you do to deal with your own aggressive tendencies? In this chapter you will learn about how you can use behavioural ideas and insights into thought patterns to help you become assertive in situations where you might be inclined to be *directly aggressive* and/or to help you modify your reactions if a more accepting or tolerant approach might work out better for you. In the second part of the chapter we will then consider what you can do to change behaviour patterns that are *indirectly aggressive*.

Aggressive behaviour

Aggressive behaviour involves seeking to have your own wishes met, irrespective of the needs or wishes of others and without showing reasonable respect. In the introduction we highlighted five examples of directly aggressive behaviour.

If you act with **direct aggression** then you may do any or all of the following things:

1. Dominate conversations, interrupt other people and not give them the opportunity to speak

2. Shout or use abusive language towards other people when they don't act in a way you agree with or they challenge what you are saying

3. Find it difficult to acknowledge your faults or errors and act defensively when criticized reasonably

4. Use intimidating body language or threats, or assault others when they do not do what you want, or as a way of trying to coerce them or express your disapproval

5. Show little regard for the rights of others and treat them without much respect

---

 Read through the above examples of directly aggressive behaviour. Which ones do you think may sometimes apply to you? Using the headings below, note down details of situations where you have a tendency to act in any of those five ways.

(a) Type of situation (e.g. work, home, social relationships, romantic relationships, dealing with people in authority).

(b) Who do you tend to act aggressively towards? (Make a note of any particular individuals with whom you are more passive.)

(c) Ways in which your behaviour is aggressive. (Which of the five examples of behaviour highlighted above are relevant?)

When trying out suggested methods from the first part of this chapter, look back at the details in your notes and apply the techniques to the situations you have highlighted.

Healthy and unhealthy anger

Aggressive behaviour is quite often fuelled by anger, but it is worth remembering that anger is not always a bad thing. For example, it may be an appropriate feeling to experience when you have been provoked or mistreated or someone has let you down. Anger can be *healthy* or *unhealthy* depending on how you express the feeling and the way you use it in the situation. Here are some of the differences:

Unhealthy anger	Healthy anger
You either deny your feelings of anger or you act aggressively towards the other person	You acknowledge and express your anger clearly but you do so in a non-violent, reasonable way
You allow your feelings about the situation to get you down	You try to act constructively, deal with the problem and learn from it
The anger gnaws away at you and you find it difficult to get rid of	Ultimately, you let go of the anger and move on
You treat the other person without respect	You treat the other person with respect even though you are angry with them

Note: A more detailed analysis of the difference between healthy and unhealthy anger can be found in David Burn's book *Ten Days to Self-Esteem* (Harper, 1993).

The ideas that follow build on the notion that changing your aggressive behaviour often involves expressing anger in a *healthy* way in line with the distinctions made above.

What if you are not sure whether your behaviour is aggressive?

You may feel that sometimes you display some of the behaviour patterns described as characteristic of aggressive behaviour, but that they are justified by the situation or by the actions of others. People have different views about how justified another person's actions are in reacting in what might be considered an aggressive way. It is not possible to lay down universally agreed rules about what constitutes aggressive behaviour, applicable to every person in every situation. In light of this, a five-step approach is recommended to tackle your own *tendencies to over-react* in particular situations and express your anger in an unhealthy way. This involves looking at your own behaviour in a *practical* way rather than becoming too preoccupied with whether it is or isn't aggressive or fair.

Changing behaviour that might be aggressive – five-step analysis

Step 1: Select a situation

Think of a past situation where your behaviour *might* have been considered aggressive. In doing this you are not required to make a judgement as to whether your behaviour actually was aggressive, it just needs to be a situation where *either* (a) you are worried that it was aggressive or (b) someone else involved or witnessing the situation might have accused you of behaving aggressively, rightly or wrongly. Write down what the situation was.

Step 2: Describe how you behaved

When you have chosen your situation, the next step is to write down how you behaved (including anything you said if the situation involved a verbal exchange).

Step 3: Describe the outcome

Write down what happened after you behaved in that way, both immediately and in terms of any longer term impact, if relevant. Also, write down any feelings or thoughts *immediately* after acting in that way and any longer term feelings or thoughts you have about the situation and how you acted.

Step 4: Imagine a calmer way in which you might have acted

Write down what you might have done differently if you had been acting more moderately.

Step 5: Consider the potential benefits and potential disadvantages of acting in that calmer way

Write down the potential pros and cons, were you to act more moderately.

Mervyn: Using the five-step analysis to act more calmly

Mervyn is in a pub and has been waiting at the bar for a few minutes to order a drink. When the person in front of him has just been served, the bar attendant calls out 'Who's next?' Just as Mervyn opens his mouth to give his order, another man pushes in front of him and asks for two pints of lager and a rum and coke.

The situation results in an exchange which later on Mervyn writes down using the five-step analysis.

Step 1: Situation
A man pushed in front of me in the pub and started ordering when it wasn't his turn.

Step 2: How I behaved
I grabbed his arm and called out loudly and angrily, 'What do you think you're doing? You've jumped the queue.'

Step 3: The outcome
He responded equally angrily, pulling my arm, glaring at me and saying 'Take your arm off me.' There was a tense situation witnessed by all the surrounding people including the friends I was with, which ultimately ended in me getting served first, but I felt angry and anxious for a while. I found it difficult to relax in the conversation with my friends afterwards and didn't sleep well that night. I wondered what might have happened if the situation had escalated further and felt guilty and worried about what my friends might think of me for leaping in.

Step 4: A calmer way I might have acted
I could have simply ignored what he was doing and let it go as it wasn't that urgent for me to get served. Alternatively, if I did want to say something I could have said calmly, 'Excuse me, I think I was here first. Do you mind if I go first?'

Step 5: Benefits and disadvantages of acting more calmly

Pros	Cons
• I might have achieved the aim of being served first without a major conflict and subsequent anxiety • He might have responded in a less aggressive way towards me • I wouldn't have got so wound up • I wouldn't have worried about what my friends thought	• He might have ignored me or disputed what I said and I might not then have got served before him, but would that really have mattered? • I might have felt a loss of face if he hadn't listened to me, but would my friends really have thought any worse of me for it? More likely they would have just thought he was a bit of an idiot for acting that way

Choosing to experiment

Once you have weighed up the pros and cons of acting in a calmer way, if you decide that the pros may outweigh the cons then make a *conscious decision* to experiment with acting in the calmer way next time a similar situation arises, where you might be provoked to act in a way which some people might consider aggressive. Try it out and if you feel better about the outcome, then congratulate yourself and keep trying it out until it becomes a positive habit!

If, on looking at the pros and cons of acting in a calmer way, you are not sure whether you would prefer to do so or you think that you would actually prefer to keep acting in the way that might be considered aggressive, still consider trying out the alternative, calmer way as an experiment to test out whether you may be wrong, unless the risks attached to doing so are obviously very serious (which in most situations is not the case). What have you got to lose from experimenting with acting in a calmer way? Why not try it? You may learn that you can act in ways that you didn't realize you could and you may see that the results are better than you expected.

 Think of a situation in which your behaviour *might* have been considered aggressive (whether or not you would label it that way, and even if you think your behaviour was justified in the situation). Write down an analysis of it using the five-step process above, then consider experimenting with a calmer way of acting if a similar situation arises.

Changing *thinking patterns* that might be aggressive

The above practical approach to changing behaviour that might be considered aggressive is essentially *behavioural* in nature. That is to say, it encourages you to try out different behaviours with the aim of gaining an improved outcome for yourself.

This kind of behavioural approach can be extended further, using the ideas of psychologist Albert Ellis, so as to include a *cognitive* element in your approach to changing aggression, i.e. you can start to look at *thinking patterns* that are often associated with your aggressive behaviour and do something about those in order to deal with your aggression at an even more fundamental level.

Two types of thinking associated with aggressive actions

In their book, *How to Keep People from Pushing Your Buttons* (Citadel Press, 1994), Albert Ellis and Arthur Lange highlight some ways in which you might think about situations that could well lead to you overreacting. In colourful language they refer to these types of thinking as 'screwball types of thinking', which conveys that they consider these belief patterns to be distorted (although most of us can readily identify with them at times!). Below are two types of such screwball thinking mentioned by Ellis and Lange, which are often involved with aggressive actions. Since they both begin with the letter 'A', you can think of them as **the two A's of aggressive thinking**.

(i) Awfulizing

This is when you imagine that the consequences of a certain event or action or situation will be awful or unbearable. (It can also be called 'catastrophizing' (see p. 102), e.g.

'I'm caught in a traffic jam, running late for a meeting. I start to think, "If don't get there on time it's going to be a disaster ... I'm going to look terrible ... Everyone there is going to think I'm a failure ..." As a result of thinking in this way, I start to get angry, hoot my car horn and start thumping my dashboard with my hand.'

(ii) Absolutist thinking

This is when you think that someone else, or you yourself, or a particular situation *must*, *should* or *has to* be or act a certain way, or that someone or something *shouldn't*, *mustn't* or *can't* be a certain way, e.g.

'My friend is rather scatterbrained, and it's beginning to get on my nerves that he doesn't seem to be able to organize his affairs properly. When I'm round at his house, I see the house is in a mess and there is a red reminder for his electricity bill on the table. He doesn't seem particularly bothered. I think, "Why doesn't he sort himself out? There's no reason why he shouldn't do so. He really ought to get his act together." I feel angry with him and speak to him in a brusque way.'

Evaluating thoughts associated with aggressive actions

Once you have identified situations in which you are awfulizing or using absolutist thinking, here is an **anger checklist** made up of three questions that you can ask yourself to help you evaluate your thoughts in the situation.

1. Are these thoughts helping me to act in a practical, sensible way?

2. Are these thoughts leading me to feel better?

3. What alternative way could I think about the situation which would be less extreme while still being accurate?

Asking myself these questions about the 'awfulizing' example above, where I react to a traffic jam by awfulizing about how disastrous it's going to be if I arrive late for my meeting and how everyone there is going to think I'm a failure, I might come up with the following answers.

1. Are these thoughts helping me to act in a practical, sensible way?
'No – these thoughts are leading me to hoot my horn and start thumping my hand on the dashboard, which isn't going to do anything to help resolve the situation and might lead me into conflict with other motorists or even the police.'

2. Are these thoughts leading me to feel better?
'No – these thoughts are simply leading me to get progressively more angry and frustrated.'

3. What alternative way could I think about the situation which would be less extreme while still being accurate?

'I could think "It's a nuisance that I'm caught in a traffic jam and am going to be late for the meeting, but it's outside my control as to whether the traffic will clear in time for me to get there, so there's no point in trying to will it to happen. If I get an opportunity to pull the car to the side and make a call to warn people that I am likely to be late, then I can do that. Otherwise, I'll just have to apologize when I get there and perhaps allow longer next time.'

Look again at the example above, relating to *absolutist thinking*. Ask yourself the three questions from the anger checklist in relation to the thoughts the person had in *that* example, and see if you can come up with an alternative way that they might think about the situation which might help them to be less aggressive in a similar situation.

Realistic references

Ellis and Lange suggest that if you find yourself indulging in awfulizing or absolutist thinking, you may well find it helpful to replace your extreme thoughts with thoughts that express what they call 'realistic preferences'.

In chapter 2, we considered the idea that expressing yourself assertively often involves taking ownership of and acknowledging your feelings and views (p. 39). The idea of realistic preferences is an extension of this. Put simply, it means that rather than use an awfulizing expression, such as 'I can't bear it', or an absolutist expression such as 'you mustn't do that', you acknowledge what you are thinking or feeling and express that thought or feeling in a realistic and more moderate way. Here are some examples.

Thought	Type of thinking involved	Substituting a realistic preference
'He can't do that'	Absolutist thinking	'I would prefer it if he didn't do that but it's not the end of the world.'
'It's a complete disaster'	Awfulizing	'I wish it hadn't happened and it's going to create some problems and embarrassment but it will pass.'

REMEMBER THIS!!! Extreme feelings and aggressive behaviour often arise because of *overreacting* and thinking in absolutist or awfulizing ways. To help yourself feel better and react more sensibly, try to express your thoughts in terms of realistic preferences or less extreme ways of thinking about a situation which are still accurate but not so inflexible or dramatic.

The following two case studies show how identifying when you are using awfulizing or absolutist thinking patterns and substituting realistic preferences or less extreme ways of thinking about the situation can help you to act differently, achieve better outcomes and feel better.

Ahmad: Using the anger checklist to stop and evaluate

Ahmad works in the IT department of a large corporation. At short notice his boss Steve asks him to prepare a training day for sales staff on using the latest software for recording and analysing transactions. Ahmad has to put aside the work he is doing. He spends the morning working on materials for the training day and devising a schedule for it. Just as he has finished and is about to resume the work he had been doing, Steve sends him a short email telling him his help is no longer required for preparing the training day, as they are going to outsource the training. Ahmad is livid. He thinks, 'This guy is a complete ***** [absolutist thinking]. I'm not going to put up with it'. He forgets about the work he was about to resume and storms off to the staff canteen, seething. Once in the canteen he pauses and reflects on his thoughts asking himself the three questions from the anger checklist.

1. Are these thoughts helping me to act in a practical, sensible way?
'No – they've just caused me to break away from what I was about to do and make poor use of my time.'

2. Are these thoughts leading me to feel better?
'No – they've just caused me to become wound up!'

3. What alternative way could I think about the situation, which would be less extreme while still being accurate?
'I could try to think in terms of a realistic preference instead of reacting dramatically, and say to myself, "I feel irritated because I've wasted a morning's work and Steve hasn't given me a proper explanation or an apology. It's a nuisance and I would prefer it if Steve were a better manager, but he's unlikely to change so I might as well just leave it."' After this reflection, Ahmad goes back and gets on with the task that he had put aside while working on the training event. He still feels irritated but he is able to shrug his shoulders. He doesn't let Steve's poor management skills get to him. (Note: in some situations, a more assertive response from Ahmad might involve him calmly explaining to Steve the inconvenience that he was caused by the aborted request, and that he would have appreciated an apology. However, in this situation Ahmad judged that such a request would not produce a helpful response from Steve, so as a sensible, practical decision he decided just to leave it and not get wound up about it).

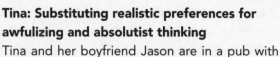

Tina: Substituting realistic preferences for awfulizing and absolutist thinking

Tina and her boyfriend Jason are in a pub with some acquaintances. Tina notices that Jason is chatting with a woman from his office in a friendly way and that from time to time he touches the woman lightly on the arm, and laughs in what Tina considers to be an intimate, flirtatious manner. She thinks, 'He is flirting and making a fool of me in full view of everyone. This is unbearable. I'm not going to put up with it *[awfulizing]*. He has no right to treat me like that. He shouldn't act that way – it's disgusting *[absolutist thinking]*.' She is about to go up and pull Jason away forcefully. Then, reflecting on how she is thinking, Tina realizes that it is making her blood boil, her face go red and her body tense up. She substitutes a realistic preference: 'I think it's very insensitive that Jason is flirting in that way and would prefer it if he didn't, but it may not have the same significance to him.' She manages to turn away and starts to focus on a conversation with someone else. Her anger and temptation to react aggressively fall away.

Think of a situation or type of situation where some people might think your behaviour is aggressive. Examine the situation and your thoughts, asking the three questions from the anger checklist. See if you can come up with some realistic preferences or less extreme ways of thinking that you can substitute in a future similar situation, in place of any awfulizing or absolutist thoughts you identify. Then try out your substitute ways of thinking when a similar situation arises and see what happens!

Indirect aggression

So far in this chapter we have considered behaviour that is directly aggressive (or on the point of becoming so). Sometimes, however, aggression is less obvious, involving indirect means to influence or control people or to disrupt or create difficulties in situations, often with a personal motive.

In the introduction we highlighted five examples of indirectly aggressive behaviour:

1. Lying or painting distorted pictures of people or situations in order to convey a particular impression or achieve results you want

2. Making out that you are a victim or have been hard done by in cases where this is not so, in order to achieve sympathy or to pressurize others into acting in certain ways

3. Playing on other people's insecurities or potential feelings of guilt, anxiety, shame or fear in order to get them to do what you would like

4. Committing to do things to achieve agreements with others even though you don't intend to carry through your commitments

5. Playing innocent or misdescribing what you have agreed to previously, so as to cover up your own part in creating a problematic situation.

Read through the above examples of indirectly aggressive behaviour. Which ones do you think may sometimes apply to you? Using the headings below, note down details of situations where you have a tendency to act in any of those five ways.

(a) Type of situation (e.g. work, home, social relationships, romantic relationships, dealing with people in authority).

(b) Who do you tend to act in this way towards? (Make a note of any particular individuals with whom you behave like this.)

(c) Ways in which your behaviour is indirectly aggressive. (Which of the five examples of behaviour highlighted above are relevant?)

When trying out suggested methods from this second part of the chapter, look back at the details in your notes and apply the techniques to the situations you have highlighted.

Three possible reasons why you might act disruptively or manipulatively

Here are three common reasons why you might act with indirect aggression (they can overlap):

(i) You believe acting manipulatively or disruptively is an effective way of getting what you want.

(ii) You are worried about what might happen if you express what you want assertively or honestly, so instead you seek to achieve what you want by covert means.

(iii) From a young age you have acted manipulatively or disruptively and it has become a habit that you find difficult to break.

We are now going to look at each of these reasons, considering whether they are valid and what you can do to help yourself act assertively if you think you have a tendency to act in a manipulative or disruptive way for any of the stated reasons.

Reason (i): You believe that acting manipulatively or disruptively is an effective way of getting what you want.

Is this valid? Sometimes you may get what you want in the short term by acting manipulatively or disruptively, but it is often at a cost. For example, you may find that as people get to know you better they start to realize that you are acting manipulatively or they may get fed up with the disruptions you cause, with the result that they start to avoid you. You may find that good friends get hurt or angry with you if they find out that you have acted deceitfully in your dealings with them. You may also find that you feel guilty after having acted in these ways because you know you have been deceitful or have created problems for others.

Suggestion: write a list of the pay-offs for you of acting manipulatively or disruptively, then against it write a list of the potential problems that may arise from acting in this way. Do the benefits from acting in this way really outweigh the potential problems? If not, then make a commitment to act more honestly next time in a similar situation. If you do still feel that there are significant pay-offs for you from acting in this way, then ask yourself if there is another way in which you could gain those benefits without having to act manipulatively or disruptively.

Rolf: Comparing benefits and problems from manipulative behaviour

Rolf and his partner, Alex, are due to go out to a party in the evening and the issue comes up as to who will drive. A discussion ensues.

Rolf: 'I've been thinking about how we're going to get to the party tonight – would you be OK driving? It's not too far.'

Alex: 'I would prefer not to – I was thinking of having a few drinks and wouldn't be able to do that if I drive.'

Rolf: 'I see, but remember the last party we went to, when you had a few too many and didn't feel too great the next day!'

Alex: 'True – but I could probably limit myself to a maximum of two or three small glasses then I'd be OK.'

Rolf: 'Yes, that would be good if you could do it, but it's a bit of a slippery slope – you remember when we went to Maxine's and you meant to have just one glass of wine, and ended up having nearly two bottles and making a fool of yourself!'

Alex: 'Oh, yes, perhaps you're right, I wouldn't want to do that again.'

Rolf: 'Yes, it was pretty bad and if you commit yourself to driving this time then you know you'll be OK, because you don't drink when you know you have to drive.'

Alex: 'True – I think I'll drive this time and stay sober.'

In the conversation, Rolf has persuaded Alex to drive them to the party by playing on his feelings of guilt about a previous drunken episode. Actually, Rolf wants to drink at the party himself and that was the main reason why he used this manipulative form of persuasion.

After Rolf has persuaded Alex to do this, he feels a bit guilty because he knows that he has acted manipulatively. He writes down the pay-offs from his manipulative behaviour and the problems from it.

Payoffs from manipulative behaviour	Problems from manipulative behaviour
I got the practical outcome I wanted – I won't have to drive to the party so I can drink	• I feel guilty • If Alex realizes that I've acted manipulatively, he will feel hurt and get annoyed with me • If I continue being manipulative in this way then it's going to be difficult to maintain genuine trust in the relationship

Reflecting on what he has written, Rolf realizes that there was probably another option he could have chosen which would have meant that he could still drink, without him persuading Alex to drive by manipulative argument: namely, he could have suggested they get a cab to and from the party so that they could both drink. He goes back to Alex and makes that suggestion, saying that if Alex wants to drink but to do so in a limited way, then maybe they can both agree a sensible drinking limit and make sure they both stick to it!

Reason (ii): You are worried about what might happen if you express what you want assertively or honestly, so instead you seek to achieve what you want by covert means.

Is this valid? It is possible that in some cases, if you were to act honestly or assertively the results would be not worth the risk. However, if you find yourself *frequently* acting manipulatively and doing so with a variety of different people, then it may well be that you are overestimating the potential problems from acting honestly and assertively.

Suggestion: Use the technique for *facing up to your fears of being assertive* from chapter 4 (p. 102) to acknowledge and assess your anxieties about acting or speaking honestly.

Gloria: Facing up to your fears of being assertive

Gloria has agreed with her friend Jean to go out to see a film on Thursday evening. Forgetting this, she agrees to go out for dinner that night with Mike whom she has been communicating with on a dating website. She would prefer to go ahead with the date with Mike but is worried about how Jean will react if she tells her the truth, so instead she plans to tell Jean the 'white lie' that she is busy at work and is not sure she will be able to get away in time on Thursday.

Gloria realizes that she is about to act deceitfully. Her reason for doing so is that she is worried about what might happen if she expresses what she wants honestly and assertively; she thinks Jean may get annoyed with her. Before she goes ahead with her 'white lie', Gloria uses the *facing up to your fears* technique to help decide what to do.

Step 1: Consider options

Gloria draws up a list of different options for how she could act and lists the advantages and disadvantages of each.

Option 1: Tell a 'white lie' about being busy at work

Advantages	Disadvantages
• If successful, then it won't look like I have chosen to let Jean down, just that I have been forced to change plans due to circumstances beyond my control	• If Jean discovers the truth, she may feel even more let down because of my deception • Jean may say she can wait and see on the day whether I'm free, in which case I will need to carry the deception a step further on the day and pretend I'm still in work

Option 2: Tell the truth that I arranged the date with Mike forgetting about my arrangement with her. Check how important it is to her to see the film on that particular day and then decide what to do based on her reaction

Advantages	Disadvantages
• I will have treated Jean with honesty	• Jean may feel I am putting pressure on her to change the arrangement
• Jean will have the opportunity to react honestly	• She may be annoyed that I forgot about the arrangement with her
• If Jean doesn't mind me rearranging with her then everybody will be happy	• I may end up having to rearrange the date with Mike depending on how Jean reacts when I tell her

Option 3: Change the arrangement with Mike – stick to original plan with Jean

Advantages	Disadvantages
• I won't be letting down Jean	• I'll never know if Jean would have been OK with me going ahead with seeing Mike and rearranging my evening with her
	• Mike may be annoyed

Step 2: Select the assertive option

Gloria decides that an assertive person would probably choose option 2.

Step 3: Face your fears

She analyses her fears using the five questions suggested in the *facing your fears* technique.

(i) What is the worst that could happen if I act assertively?
'Jean may get annoyed.'

(ii) How likely as a percentage is it to happen?
'Knowing Jean, it's actually unlikely that she'll get very annoyed. There is probably a 50 per cent chance that she may initially be a little *irritated* that I'm asking her to rearrange, but there is an equal possibility that another day would be just as good for her and that it won't be a problem to rearrange. She may even be pleased to hear that I've got a second date with Mike.'

(iii) Is there anything I can do to reduce that percentage?
'If I apologize sincerely that may help to reduce the likelihood of her getting irritated.'

(iv) If it does happen will it still be worth me having acted assertively?
'Yes, probably because otherwise I'll never know what would have happened if I'd spoken to her honestly.'

(v) What can I do to deal with it if it does happen?
'If Jean does get irritated, I'll say I understand and stick with the arrangement with her and change the date with Mike.'

Step 4: Decide how you are going to act

Reflecting on her options and her analysis of the worst case, Gloria decides that it is worth taking the risk of speaking honestly and assertively to Jean in this situation. To help bolster her confidence to do this, she reminds herself of the potential advantages.

Step 5: Act

Gloria does speak honestly to Jean. It turns out that Jean was actually wondering about changing the day anyway as the Friday would be a better day for her for seeing the film, so they agree to go out on the Friday instead and Gloria sees Mike on the Thursday. Gloria is relieved she didn't engage in the 'white lie' she had planned and that the situation worked out well for both of them.

Reason (iii): From a young age you have acted manipulatively or disruptively and it has become a habit that you find difficult to break.

Is this valid? This can arise if, for example, you were brought up to believe that you shouldn't act in certain ways. It could also arise from gender, social or religious expectations. You may have been socialized into believing that you shouldn't voice your opinions or react assertively, or that it is rude or self-centred to do so. Instead you have got into an automatic habit of trying to achieve what you want in indirect ways, by manipulation, by playing the victim or by creating a scene. Alternatively, you may have grown up in an environment where success was highly praised and failure was regarded as unacceptable, so rather than admit to failings honestly you try to deny or deflect responsibility. This explanation for habitual manipulative behaviour relates to the moral and cultural expectations or rules of conduct that you have absorbed from a young age.

The rules of conduct that you have learned from a young age may *seem* right or natural to you, because you have held them for so long, but it does not necessarily mean they have any objective validity. Being assertive is about starting to make your own decisions in a responsible, reasonable way rather than following set roles without challenging them.

Suggestion: Remind yourself of any rights and responsibilities that may apply to your situation (see chapter 1) and identify what would be an *assertive* way of acting in the situation, bearing in mind those rights and responsibilities. Try acting that way the next time the situation comes along.

CASE STUDY

Patricia: Reminding yourself of your rights and responsibilities instead of acting manipulatively or disruptively

Patricia works as a support worker in a housing association for young women with mental health problems. She is assigned to help one particular young woman, Tracy, who has a likeable and quite mischievous personality. One night, Tracy stays out of the house beyond the required curfew time and sneaks back in late. Patricia knows about it but doesn't report it to the manager or take any action, because she likes Tracy and doesn't want her to get into trouble. The manager finds out and when supervising Patricia explains to her that it is important to maintain disciplinary boundaries with the residents and be consistent with them all for several reasons, including that other residents may rightly feel aggrieved, and that the curfew is there for a reason to maintain discipline and ensure safety. Patricia's reaction is to start crying and say that maybe she is not suitable for the job and she knows that the manager must think she is useless.

In this situation, Patricia is playing a poor, helpless individual in order to sidestep being disciplined or facing censure. She does this rather than react defensively or with direct aggression to the criticism, because from a young age she was taught that it is unfeminine to react aggressively. Instead, her tendency is to do the opposite and try to appear weak or unworldly when criticized for acting unprofessionally. The result in this case isn't positive for her: her manager gets frustrated with her and Patricia feels quite isolated. When she reflects afterwards on her rights and responsibilities (see chapter 1), she realizes that she has a right to make mistakes and the responsibility to make decisions. She decides to commit to trying to take more personal responsibility for her decisions in a future situation and to acknowledge when she has made a mistake, which is a much more assertive way of acting in this kind of situation. It proves a challenge for her, but over time she is able to win back the trust and support of her manager.

If you think that you have a tendency to act disruptively or manipulatively, then reflect on whether any of the three reasons above apply to your behaviour, and try out the relevant suggestion(s) for challenging and addressing your behaviour when a typical situation arises.

Key ideas from chapter 5

Some of the key ideas from chapter 5 are:

- Aggressive behaviour involves seeking to have your own wishes met, irrespective of the needs or wishes of others and without showing reasonable respect

- Aggression can be *direct*, through such forms as verbal abuse or physical aggression, or *indirect*, through manipulating situations or people in a disruptive or dishonest way

- Anger can be healthy or unhealthy depending on how you express it and the way you use it

- You can use the five-step analysis (p. 128) to help you act in a calmer way in situations where you have a tendency to be directly aggressive

- You can use the anger checklist (pp. 134–5) and substitute realistic preferences (p. 136) to help you deal with 'awfulizing' or 'absolutist' thinking patterns that are causing you to become wound up

- In situations where you tend to act manipulatively or disruptively, consider whether your reasons for doing so fit into any of the three patterns highlighted in pages 143–153, then use the suggested techniques to examine your reasoning.

6. Self-esteem and assertiveness

Assertiveness represents a reasonable middle path between being passive and being aggressive. In the last two chapters, we have looked at ways of changing passive and aggressive behaviour. These non-assertive ways of behaving are quite often linked to your level of self-esteem, that is, the extent to which you value yourself. If you are inclined to *under*value yourself, doubt your own abilities and pay too much attention to the views of others, you may have a tendency to behave passively. If you tend to *over*-value yourself, overestimate your abilities and pay too little attention to the views of others, you may have a tendency to behave aggressively. In this chapter we will consider first what to do if low self-esteem is leading you to behave passively, and secondly what to do if you have unduly high self-esteem which is leading you to behave dismissively or aggressively towards others.

Low self-esteem and passive behaviour

If you do not believe in your own abilities and worth, then you are likely to hesitate to take assertive actions in your relationships because:

1. You may doubt your own abilities to be assertive and successful in relationships, or you may feel that your character is such that you cannot be assertive.

2. You may blame yourself if any negative consequences ensue or doubt yourself further if you don't succeed.

3. You may doubt your right to behave assertively.

Some of the techniques we have already looked into can help you to deal with item 2, fears about negative consequences (see chapter 4, p. 97ff), and item 3, doubts about your rights (see chapter 1). In the first part of this chapter we will focus on item 1, what to do if you doubt your own abilities or believe that your own character is such that behaving assertively is not possible for you.

Limiting beliefs

A **limiting belief** is a general belief that you hold, whether stated or not, that reduces your ability to achieve what you want to achieve. There are a number of different types of limiting belief. Here we will focus on two types of limiting belief that are relevant to assertiveness.

Two types of limiting belief	Examples
Limiting beliefs about your abilities	'I won't succeed' 'I am useless at relationships' 'I am always wrong'
Limiting beliefs about your characteristics	'I am stupid' 'I am self-centred' 'I am a failure'

It is easy to see how limiting beliefs may lead you to behave passively. Here is an example.

Limiting belief: 'I am useless at relationships'

↓

Consequences: I doubt myself when I enter into new relationships. I assume they are not going to work and I become anxious.

↓

Behaviour: Fearing and expecting a poor result, I try not to do anything that I think might upset relationships and I end up behaving passively instead of assertively.

There may be aspects of a limiting belief that have a degree of truth, but exaggerating that element of truth into a general belief about yourself in all situations is often what is harmful. If you find yourself over-generalizing in negative ways about yourself then try to reframe your negative self-talk in a more specific, less universal way and with a constructive approach. For example, instead of saying to yourself, 'I am useless at relationships', you might say to yourself, 'My last relationship didn't work out and with hindsight I can see that was probably partly due to how I acted. Next time I will try to act differently.'

Dealing with limiting beliefs

Here is a three-step process for dealing with limiting beliefs.

Step 1: Identifying your limiting beliefs
Step 2: Changing limiting beliefs
Step 3: Testing out your new beliefs

Step 1: Identifying your limiting beliefs

(a) Listing limiting beliefs you are aware of

It may be that you can already think of some limiting beliefs about your abilities or your characteristics in certain contexts or more generally. If so, then for step 1 simply start by listing some of them and the type of situation where they create difficulties for you. Here is an example.

What is the limiting belief about your abilities or characteristics?	In what type of situation does it cause problems?	What types of problem does it cause?
'I'm not good enough to get a job I like'	Work situations when attending job interviews or seeking promotion in a job I'm in	I lack motivation to apply for jobs/ promotions or I perform badly in job interviews
'I'm always unlucky'	Most situations!	I don't look out for opportunities or take advantage of them because I don't believe they will work out
'I'm a poor parent'	Situations where it would be sensible to encourage my children to stay within reasonable boundaries in their behaviour	I tend to let my children do whatever they say they want to do as I doubt my ability to impose boundaries or provide appropriate discipline

Characteristics of limiting beliefs that inhibit assertiveness

If you have a tendency to behave passively and not assert yourself enough, then in looking for a limiting belief that might be relevant to your assertiveness, look for the following features:

- A belief that is negative about your character or abilities

- A belief that is dogmatic, i.e. it is something that you don't think to challenge or that you regard as always true (or true so often that it's not worth challenging)

- A belief that in some respects is inhibiting you from making the most of your opportunities or expressing your views or feelings clearly or sufficiently.

(b) Identifying limiting beliefs from negative self-talk
If you are not able to list limiting beliefs straight away, then a technique you can use to find them is to observe your thoughts. When you catch yourself thinking negatively about yourself or your prospects, ask yourself if there is a general limiting belief about your abilities or your characteristics which crops up repeatedly or underlies a particular negative thought, e.g.

1. Situation: Going out on a date
2. Negative thought: 'They won't like me'
3. Possible limiting belief: 'I'm an uninteresting person'

In the above example, the possible limiting belief 'I'm an uninteresting person' might be leading to the particular negative thought 'They won't like me'. Of course, different people may have a different limiting belief that applies to them in this kind of situation. Other possible limiting beliefs in the above situation might be, 'Things never work out for me' or 'I'm unlucky when it comes to romance'.

(c) The downward arrow technique

If you can identify some individual negative thoughts or predictions in particular situations but still have difficulty identifying the particular limiting belief(s) relating to them, you can try using the so-called 'downward arrow technique' (also known as the vertical arrow technique) to establish what the limiting belief(s) may be.

To use this technique you take a self-critical or anxious thought or prediction that you are thinking, and then ask yourself, 'What does that mean?' or 'What does that show?'. You keep doing that with each answer you give, until you reach a point which you feel reflects the limiting belief that underlies the thought.

Depending on the context you can also use other variations for the question that you use, similar to the questions described above, such as 'So what?', or 'What's so bad about that?', or 'Why does that matter?', or 'What does that say about me?', to help get to the limiting belief.

To help find your limiting beliefs try applying the downward arrow technique to a situation where you feel strongly negative about yourself or about something you have or haven't achieved – strong negative emotion about yourself can be an indicator that there may be a limiting belief involved.

CASE STUDY

Nick: Using the downward arrow technique to find limiting beliefs

Nick's boss is going away to a conference and has asked Nick to chair a meeting in his absence.

Nick starts to get very anxious about the prospect that he may not chair the meeting very well. He uses the downward arrow technique to trace the underlying limiting belief behind his negative thought pattern.

Negative thought: 'I expect I'll make a mess of the meeting.'
Question: 'So what?'
Answer: 'The other people there may think I've done a bad job.'
Question: 'Why does that matter?'
Answer: 'They may laugh at me behind my back'
Question: 'What would that show?'
Answer: 'I'm not likeable.' *[limiting belief]*

Different people using the downward arrow technique may find that they have different limiting beliefs to Nick's in a similar situation. Someone else might, for example, find that for them the underlying limiting belief was, 'I'll never be a success'. To determine what your own limiting beliefs are you need to do the exercise for yourself.

TRY IT NOW! Think back to a situation where you felt strongly negative about yourself and use the downward arrow technique to try to establish if there were limiting beliefs involved and, if so, what they might have been.

If your self-critical thought is a negative prediction about yourself, as in the case study of Nick above, or an instruction to yourself that you should or should not do something, then ask yourself *why* you think you won't achieve in the particular instance, or ask yourself *why* you should not act in a particular way. That may help you to clarify what the underlying limiting self-beliefs are.

Step 2: Changing limiting beliefs

Having identified one or more limiting beliefs that you have, start to explore whether there are alternative beliefs that you could reasonably hold which might help you to act more assertively. Since your limiting beliefs are likely to be quite deeply entrenched, you may find that seeking alternatives and starting to act according to them takes some effort. To help you identify and start to implement alternative beliefs, you might consider possible alternative beliefs by going through the checklist of questions below.

Checklist for exploring alternatives to limiting beliefs

1. What would be a less extreme belief (or beliefs) that I might hold?

2. What would be the advantages for me of following the new, less extreme belief(s) rather than the limiting belief(s)?

3. What would be the potential disadvantages for me of holding the new belief(s) instead of the old one(s)?

4. What can I do to help me deal with the potential disadvantages of holding the new belief(s)?

Nick (continued): Exploring alternatives to limiting beliefs

Having identified a limiting belief ('I'm not likeable') from reflecting on his anxiety about making a mess of chairing the meeting in place of his boss, Nick asks himself the questions in the checklist and comes up with the following answers:

1. What would be less extreme beliefs that I might hold?

- 'Some people like me, some people don't, just as I like some people but not others'
- 'It's normal not to be liked by everyone.'

2. What would be the advantages for me of following out the new belief(s) rather than the limiting belief?
Nick comes up with the following answers:

- 'I would feel less pressurized in the meeting and less anxious'
- 'I might chair the meeting better through being more relaxed'
- 'Even if I don't chair it very well, I won't beat myself up so much about it'
- 'I won't feel the need to overprepare for the meeting, instead I can get on with other tasks or do other things I want to do.'

3. What would be the potential disadvantages for me of holding the new belief(s) instead of the old ones?
Nick comes up with the following answers:

- 'I might be pretending that I'm more likeable than I really am'
- 'It might be a sign of arrogance to think of myself as likeable.'

4. What can I do to help me deal with the potential disadvantages of holding the new belief(s)?
Nick comes up with the following answers:

- 'Remind myself that I'm not suggesting that *everyone* likes me, simply that some people do'

- 'Remind myself that I know that's true, because I have a number of friends who enjoy doing things with me and value my friendship.'

Step 3: Testing out your new beliefs

Just as Nick has some ambivalence about adopting the alternative beliefs about himself, because he is worried about pretending to be something he isn't or becoming arrogant, so you may find that you are not sure if your new beliefs are something you can commit to. The best way to find out is to *experiment*. In an appropriate situation, remind yourself of your new alternative beliefs when your habitual limiting beliefs come up, and then try to act in accordance with those beliefs. See what happens. If the results are good, then continue doing it. If they are not as good as you would hope, then try adjusting your alternative beliefs to see if there are other ones that you can adopt which do work for you.

To assess the results of your experiment in thinking differently, keep a record of the results.

Nick (continued): Testing out new beliefs
Nick keeps a record of how he gets on when he tries out his alternative beliefs.

1. Problem situation	2. Initial limiting beliefs	3. Alternative beliefs	4. Result of reminding myself of the alternative beliefs
Being asked to chair a meeting in place of my boss	'I'm not likeable'	• 'Some people like me, some people don't, just as I like some people but not others' • 'It's normal not to be liked by everyone'	I relaxed more before the meeting and during it. I spoke more purposefully in the meeting and then started looking round observing how people were reacting in the meeting, instead of keeping my head down and mumbling. Some people listened and took part actively in the meeting. Others didn't seem to be listening at all, but then they didn't seem to listen when others spoke either! I didn't take it personally. I reminded myself that that could happen to anyone. I felt quite proud after the meeting that I'd got through it well.

TRY IT NOW! Once you have created some alternative beliefs for the situation where a limiting belief is causing you to act passively, remind yourself of them in the situation and record the results, using a recording format similar to the one used by Nick.

Creating personal affirmations

If you suffer from low self-esteem, you may also find it helpful to you to remind yourself of the positive qualities that you do have or things that you have achieved. There are a number of ways of creating a list of your positive qualities and achievements. This list is often called a list of personal affirmations. If you have difficulty, one way of doing it is to ask yourself, 'What would my friends or family say were good qualities of mine, or things that I have achieved?' Write those down to start off your list of good points. If there are any other things that you are proud of, then add those to your list. Remember, the list doesn't have to involve great acts or heroics, it just needs to include things that *you* are proud of. Here is a **sample set of personal affirmations**.

'I have a number of good friends.'
'I am trustworthy.'
'I am loyal.'
'I have a good sense of humour.'
'I can drive.'
'I have brought up three children whom I love.'

Once you have written down your list of affirmations, read them through each day or when you are giving yourself a hard time and experiencing self-critical thoughts, to help you to value yourself appropriately.

 If you have difficulty in believing your affirmations, then alongside each one, write down something that is evidence of it as a reminder that it is genuine. For example, your evidence for saying 'I am loyal' might be that friends tell you that, or that you stuck by someone in a difficult situation.

The three-step process for dealing with limiting beliefs and the idea of creating personal affirmations are just two methods for developing your self-esteem. Detailed discussion of a range of additional ideas for improving low self-esteem can be found in another book in this series: *Introducing Self-Esteem: A Practical Guide.*

Excessive self-esteem and aggressive behaviour

In the preceding section we looked at how, if you have *too little self-esteem*, it can incline you to act too passively. The opposite can also be the case: it is possible to have *too high an opinion of yourself* or your abilities, and that can lead you to act aggressively or dismissively. There is some research that suggests that people who participate in potentially dangerous activities (such as driving too fast or after having consumed too much alcohol) are statistically more likely to have high self-esteem than low self-esteem, and that people involved in delinquency or violent crime may also be more likely to have high self-esteem than low self-esteem. A possible explanation of this is that high self-esteem can merge into arrogance, conceit, or disrespect for others. The best approach is probably to aim to have a *reasonable* level of self-esteem, but not too much!

When does high self-esteem become excessive?

High self-esteem need not be a problem. Indeed, it can help you to be productive and resourceful. It becomes a potential problem, however, if it leads you to dismiss or disregard the feelings of others inappropriately, or if your own estimate of your abilities is exaggerated so that you misjudge what you can realistically achieve.

Some people would argue that a person who has an excessively high opinion of themselves has *pseudo self-esteem* or *false self-esteem*, rather than genuine self-esteem. It doesn't really matter which way you describe it – the point being made is that if you think too highly of yourself and ignore or dismiss others too easily, then this may create difficulties.

Patterns of arrogance

KEY TERMS

Self-elevation, minimizing and low frustration tolerance are three types of excessive regard for yourself, or lack of regard for others, that can lead to aggressive or dismissive behaviour that is hurt-ful to others and may create practical problems.

Self-elevation is when you have an inflated belief about your own abilities or importance, e.g. thinking that you will always succeed or that others cannot do without you or that you rarely make mistakes or are invariably right.

Potential problems – you may:

- Find it difficult to cope with failure

- Blame others for your failures

- Take on more than is realistic, stress yourself out and criticize others for not helping

- Insist you are right when there are reasonable alter-native points of view or ways of looking at a situation.

Minimizing is when you adopt an attitude and approach which involves downplaying, or ignore the potentially nega-tive impacts of your actions on others so as to justify your-self, e.g. thinking that your actions towards someone don't matter, because they deserve it or because if you hadn't said what you did someone else would have done so.

Potential problems – in giving yourself licence to say what you want and do what you want towards others you may:

- Hurt others unnecessarily
- Encourage conflict
- Lose respect from others in relationships.

Low frustration tolerance is when you regard it as terrible if others get in the way of you achieving your aims or wishes or if you personally don't achieve your aims, e.g. losing patience with yourself or others when things don't go as you would like.

Potential problems – you can be unduly dismissive of others and/or angry with yourself or with a situation that doesn't work out the way you want it to.

Dealing with arrogant belief patterns

Here is a four-step process for addressing your own potentially arrogant belief patterns.

Step 1: Identify a potential problem situation
Step 2: Examine your justification for how you acted
Step 3: Ask how you could react differently next time
Step 4: Try out your new actions

Step 1: Identify a potential problem situation

In chapter 5, when we discussed changing aggressive behaviour by acting more calmly (pp. 128–132), you were encouraged to begin by focusing on selecting a situation where your behaviour *might* be considered aggressive. Similarly here, for step 1 you should begin by thinking of a situation where you *might* have been arrogant or self-centred. This could either be a situation where (a) you personally are worried that you were arrogant, or (b) where someone else involved or witnessing the situation might have accused you of being arrogant.

Step 2: Examine your justification for how you acted

In step 2, describe how you acted in the situation and what *justification* you might now give for acting in that way in the situation. Then consider your justification and answer the three **questions** below to help decide whether you were acting in an arrogant way.

(i) Am I exaggerating the significance or importance of my own needs being met in the situation (self-elevation)?

(ii) Am I downplaying the potentially negative impacts of my actions on others or my own role in creating the situation (minimizing)?

(iii) Am I exaggerating how terrible it would be if others stop me achieving my aims or if personally I am unsuccessful in achieving them (low frustration tolerance)?

Step 3: Ask how you could react differently next time

If in step 2 you decided that you were not exaggerating, minimizing or showing low frustration tolerance *at all* in the justification you have given for acting in the way you did, then this suggests that on reflection you do not think that you were acting inappropriately. However, if in your answers to any of the three questions in step 2 you did acknowledge that your justification involved exaggerating, minimizing or low frustration tolerance, then ask yourself how you could react differently next time.

Step 4: Try out your new reactions

When a similar situation arises try, reacting in the new way that you decided on in step 3 and see if it produces better results or if you feel better after reacting in that new way.

Alice: Using the four-step process for dealing with arrogant belief patterns

Alice plans a holiday with her family for half term. A couple of weeks before half term she approaches her boss to ask her for holiday leave during half term. Her boss, Wendy, says that unfortunately two other colleagues have already booked time off during that week, so she is not able to give Alice permission to take leave then. Alice is angry, gives her boss a cold stare (aggressive behaviour) and walks out of the room.

Alice later follows the four-step process described above.

Step 1: Identify a potential problem situation
Alice realizes that some people might think her behaviour arrogant or self-centred and therefore decides to reflect on how she acted in this situation.

Step 2: Examine your justification for how you acted
Alice *justifies* her reaction to herself reasoning. 'There was no need for Wendy to stop me having a holiday then. She loves controlling people and got a kick out of saying "no". This is going to be a nightmare for me to reorganize the holiday. I really badly need a holiday and now I won't be able to sort anything out until the school holidays.'

Alice examines her justification by answering the three questions.

(i) Am I exaggerating the significance or importance of my own needs being met in the situation (self-elevation)?
Alice's answer: 'Not really, it is going to be a nightmare because Harry [Alice's husband] will be annoyed and we'll probably lose our deposit on the holiday and have to rebook another time.'

(ii) Am I downplaying the potentially negative impacts of my actions on others or my own role in creating the situation?

Alice's answer: 'Yes, I am a bit. If I'd asked Wendy a couple of months ago for the leave, she might have given it to me. I guess it did leave her with quite a difficult dilemma as two others had already booked leave.'

(iii) *Am I exaggerating how terrible it would be if others stop me achieving my aims or if personally I am unsuccessful in achieving them (low frustration tolerance)?*
Alice's answer: 'I guess I am a bit. It will be a nuisance to reorganize and we will probably lose our deposit on the holiday, but I will be able to cope. It's true Wendy can be a bit controlling, but I can't really blame her for not wanting three people off work at the same time.'

Step 3: Ask how you could react differently next time

Alice asks herself how she could act differently next time. She concludes that: 'Next time I could pause when I don't get the answer I want and try to respond calmly, asking if there is any way to resolve the situation and explaining the difficulties for me. If that doesn't produce a solution, there is no point in staring and walking off as it's just going to aggravate things, but in future it may make sense if I speak to Wendy earlier about my proposed holiday dates and check that I can take leave then, before booking anything.'

Step 4: Try out your new reactions

Alice acts differently the following year by booking holiday leave for half-term well in advance with Wendy (and before she has paid the deposit), so she doesn't have to test out reacting differently to a refusal of holiday leave. However, if she had still been refused holiday leave even when giving good notice, she might then try out her planned calm reaction of responding and seeking a resolution. This wouldn't be guaranteed to succeed but it would probably have a greater prospect of success than staring and leaving the room.

 If you are worried that you may react arrogantly sometimes, then complete the four-step process (p. 173ff) for examining a situation where you might have acted arrogantly and trying to learn lessons from it.

 Key ideas from chapter 6
Key ideas to remember from chapter 6 are:

- Low self-esteem can be linked to behaving passively

- Excessively high self-esteem can lead to arrogance and dismissive or aggressive behaviour

- If you have low self-esteem, you can use a three-step process for dealing with limiting beliefs about your abilities or worth that may be inhibiting you from acting assertively (p. 159)

- The 'downward arrow technique' (p. 162) can help you to identify your limiting beliefs

- Explore and test out alternative beliefs to help you change passive behaviour linked to low self-esteem (pp. 164–169)

- Creating a list of personal affirmations can help you to value yourself appropriately

- If your problem is unduly high self-esteem leading to arrogance, examine whether any of the three patterns of arrogance – self-elevation, minimizing or low frustration tolerance – apply to you in particular situations and try reacting differently if they do (p. 172ff).

Conclusion: Creating your own assertiveness plan

In the preceding chapters we have covered a number of aspects of assertiveness:

- Recognizing and acting on your rights and responsibilities
- Communicating effectively
- Assertiveness techniques
- How to overcome tendencies to behave passively
- How to moderate tendencies to be aggressive.

The final piece in the jigsaw of developing assertiveness involves identifying the areas where you personally want to develop, the outcomes that you would like to achieve and the techniques that you are going to try out in order to help to move towards them, and then putting these together in an assertiveness plan that you can use to guide and monitor your progress. Here are two examples of plans that might be created using simple ideas from this book.

Jenny: Creating an assertiveness plan to address shyness and doubts about expressing yourself

Jenny is someone who is capable in her work and well liked, but can be quite shy and hesitant or silent in conversations. She incorporates the ideas from this book that are most relevant to her to create an assertiveness plan, which she sets out as shown below.

Assertiveness plan

Name: Jenny

DESIRED OUTCOMES (Medium term)
- To improve my conversational skills
- To express my views more when with friends or in other social gatherings.

Problem area 1
My shyness inhibits me from building conversations

Actions to try out
- Try using self-disclosure and following up on free information (p. 37) to help with the flow of conversation
- Remember not to apologize excessively or overjustify my actions (p. 42)
- Show an interest in others by using the listening skills of paraphrasing, summarizing and reflection (p. 35)

Problem area 2
Expressing my views in social situations – I tend to think my opinions aren't worth anything or that others will dislike me if I disagree with them

Actions to try out

- Remind myself that I have a right to express my feelings and opinions and a right to make mistakes (pp. 14–15), and decide to try to enjoy social events regardless of what happens
- Express an opinion using 'I' statements and making it clear that it is a personal view (p. 39)
- If I start to worry that other people will dislike me if I disagree with them, remind myself of what I might say to someone else in my situation [useful tip for challenging passive thinking – (p. 98)]
- Challenge my own negative thoughts using the challenge checklist (p. 97) and remind myself of a more moderate belief about people's possible responses, such as 'Some people may disagree with me, but others may agree and anyway, some people may find it more interesting if there is a difference of opinion than if everyone agrees'
- Use the *face your fears* technique (p. 103ff) to help me identify how an assertive person might act and then try acting in that way

Problem area 3

Low self-esteem

Actions to try out

- Create a list of personal affirmations (p. 169) and read them through daily or when feeling self-critical.

Jenny's progress

In order to give yourself the best chance of making the changes that you are aiming for, it is important to monitor how you get on when you try out your actions. You can do this, for example, by making a note each time of anything that worked well and anything that you want to try differently, or you might review your assertiveness plan on a weekly basis and adjust it then.

In Jenny's case she uses a diary to record what she does and how she deals with the negative thoughts that occur, using the ideas from her plan. The first time she consciously attempts to express her views more in a social situation she is very nervous, but she finds some of the reminders she gives herself helpful: the reminder that she has a right to express her thoughts and feelings, and the reminder of what she might say to a friend in that situation – namely, that her views are interesting. She voices her opinions more and receives some positive feedback. She keeps up with trying the options and adjusts them as time goes on. After a while, she starts to feel more confident and people start to comment positively on her more active participation in conversations. It doesn't always work out in the way she intended, but overall she is very pleased with the outcome and that she has taken the step of contributing more and expressing herself more.

CASE STUDY

Paul: Creating an assertiveness plan to address aggressive behaviour

Paul's problem is very different from Jenny's. His tendency is to be aggressive in certain situations rather than passive. He finds himself tending to *shout* and *demand* that people do things when they are a bit slow or lazy, particularly in his work. He creates his own assertiveness plan, building on techniques for changing his aggressive behaviour.

Assertiveness plan

Name: Paul

DESIRED OUTCOMES (Medium term)

- To be more relaxed and less aggressive
- To have more constructive relationships with people

Problem area 1

Reacting impatiently to colleagues at work who are doing things slowly or in a disorganized manner

Actions to try out

- Act more calmly (chapter 5, p. 129), by asking others without raising my voice if they can try to be a bit more organized in particular ways and explaining how it

---

will help. If the opportunity arises, try out the *roll with resistance* technique for challenging what other people are doing (chapter 2, p. 47)

- Substitute a realistic preference ('I would prefer it if they acted in a more organized way, but I can't force them to') for my absolutist thinking ('They've really got to start being more organized and disciplined'), (chapter 5, p. 136)

Problem area 2
Shouting at others or acting dismissively towards them when I disagree with them, or think they've acted in an incompetent or unhelpful way

Actions to try out
- Remind myself that other people have a right to be treated with respect and to make mistakes (chapter 1, p. 15)

- Use the assertion sandwich technique (p. 45) to make constructive criticisms instead of putting people down

- If I have spoken more constructively and it still doesn't produce a good practical result, then try to 'let go' of the situation afterwards by reminding myself that other people are responsible for making their own decisions (chapter 1, p. 15). If all works out well, then relax and keep up with trying to act calmly and constructively

Paul's progress

Paul tries out the options in his assertiveness plan. He doesn't formally keep a record of how he gets on but he starts to notice that as he comes to think in a more realistic, less demanding way and to act more calmly, he achieves his objective of being more relaxed and his relationships become more enjoyable.

Using this book to create your own assertiveness plan

Having reached the end of the book, you are now in a position to create your own specific assertiveness plan in the way that Jenny and Paul did above, by reflecting on the outcomes that you personally want to achieve, the problem situations that you personally face and the particular techniques from the book that you would like to try out to help towards them.

In creating your own assertiveness plan, bear in mind the following **general considerations**:

- Assertiveness involves expressing yourself and standing up for your rights in a reasonable way

- Assertiveness is a sensible middle path between being passive (not giving yourself enough respect) and being aggressive (not giving others enough respect)

- Assertiveness involves making choices about how you act. Your thought patterns also play an important part in determining what choices you make about whether to act passively, assertively or aggressively

- If in the past you have tended to act *passively*, then a sensible aim for you is likely to be to try to act/speak *more* or *in a more noticeable way*

- If in the past you have tended to act *aggressively*, then a sensible aim for you is likely to be to try to act/speak *less* or *in a calmer way*

- The most helpful approach to assertiveness involves looking at particular situations. What is a sensible assertive choice for you will depend on:
  - The context
  - The practical options open to you
  - The outcomes you want to achieve
  - What might help or hinder you in achieving those outcomes.

In **choosing actions for your assertiveness plan**, it is important to be specific in stating the techniques that you are going to try out or the new behaviour that you are going to try to show. This helps you to focus and be clear about what you are doing. The actions you choose also need to be relevant to the problem situation that you are addressing and the overall outcomes that you want to work towards, just as they are in the plans of Jenny and Paul above.

Here is a **reminder of the different techniques that we have covered in this book**. Before you create your own assertiveness plan, read through the list to refresh your mind and decide what is most relevant for you, and then select and refer to those which are most applicable as you create the actions for your own plan.

Chapter 1: Rights and responsibilities
- Applying the four rights and responsibilities principles – p. 14ff

Chapter 2: Communicating effectively
- Using paraphrasing, summarizing and reflecting to listen effectively – p. 35

- Using free information and self-disclosure to develop conversations – p. 37

- Using 'I' statements to take ownership of your feelings, thoughts and opinions – p. 39

- Do's and don'ts of expressing yourself assertively – p. 42

- Assertive body language – p. 43

- Using an assertion sandwich to express criticism constructively – p. 45

- Challenging others by commenting on actions rather than character – p. 47

Fill in your own assertiveness plan using the template opposite and selecting relevant techniques from the contents of this book to help you towards your desired outcomes.

Assertiveness plan

Name:

Date:

DESIRED OUTCOMES (Medium term)

-
-

Problem area

Actions to try out

-
-
-
-
-
-

Appendix 1: Key developments in assertiveness training

In this appendix, we look into some of the key figures and books in the development of assertiveness training ideas.

Andrew Salter

Andrew Salter was a hypnotist and behaviour therapist (1914–1966) who is usually regarded as the first person to create a system of assertiveness training, although he did not use the actual phrase 'assertiveness' to describe his methods. He set out his ideas in his book, *Conditioned Reflex Therapy (1949)*.

The inhibitory personality

Salter used the phrase 'the inhibitory personality' to describe people with a set of tendencies to behaviour which would probably now be regarded as characteristically 'passive', such as:

- Avoiding expressing your own views
- Being frequently apologetic
- Not making demands or requests of others
- Being indecisive
- Being very self-conscious
- Placing a great importance on being accepted by others.

He argued that inhibitory behaviour is the result of conditioning children into feeling that they shouldn't express their views and punishing or criticizing them if they do so. In his view and on the basis of his work with his clients, Salter considered inhibitory behaviour not to be conducive to happiness. He felt that if you act in an inhibited way and don't express yourself, then you are likely to be constantly anxious.

The excitatory personality

By contrast, Salter praised people with an 'excitatory personality', the characteristics of which he saw as being such a tendency to behaviour such as:

- Acting spontaneously
- Expressing yourself directly and clearly
- Taking constructive action when confronted with a problem
- Making quick decisions and liking responsibility.

Salter applauded these kinds of behaviour as being illustrative of *emotional honesty*, which was the approach he encouraged people to adopt. He suggested six techniques for increasing excitation, i.e. for adopting an excitatory way of behaving rather than an inhibitory way of behaving, so as to live a happier, less anxious and more productive life. The six techniques that Salter advocated were:

1. Feeling talk
This involves expressing feelings about situations and events rather than neutrally describing them. For example, rather than simply say 'It's a sunny day', you might express some emotion about it: 'What a lovely sunny day!' or 'Great, it's sunny today!'.

2. Facial talk
This involves showing how you are feeling with your facial expressions, rather than trying to disguise this or not revealing it. For example, you might furrow your brow if puzzled or smile if amused by something.

3. Contradict and attack
In line with his overarching principle of honesty, Salter recommended voicing your disagreement with someone rather than pretending you agree when you do not.

4. The deliberate use of the word 'I'
Salter recommended using the word 'I' as much as possible, expressing your wishes, thoughts and observations with the personal pronoun: 'I did …', 'I think that …', 'I would like…', etc.

5. Expressing agreement when you are praised
Salter encouraged you to acknowledge and agree with praise rather than to dismiss it, ignore it or feel ashamed of it. It can be a feature of people with a tendency to

behave passively that they are reluctant to accept or believe praise.

6. Improvization
Salter's final basic technique was to advise you not to plan, but to act spontaneously and live for the minute. This can be helpful in situations where you have a tendency to overplan or deliberate too much, fuelling your anxiety, although there may be other occasions where some planning is useful!

Some of Salter's ideas, such as the theme of emotional honesty and the use of the word 'I' to acknowledge and take ownership of your views, feelings and thoughts are consistent with ideas about assertiveness that are now standard, and have been incorporated with the suggestions in this book. Other ideas such as his advice to act spontaneously, while they might be helpful in some situations and for some people, are not necessarily always so. It is also probably the case that his ideas have more application to dealing with passive behaviour than to modifying aggressive behaviour.

Joseph Wolpe
Like Salter, Joseph Wolpe (1915–1997) believed that anxiety was a key problem in leading to lack of assertiveness, and that behavioural conditioning techniques (helping you to practise assertive behaviour repeatedly and with success) would assist people in overcoming assertiveness difficulties created by anxiety. Wolpe is often credited with introducing the term 'assertiveness' into general use.

Affectionate expression and oppositional expression

In his work *The Practice of Behavior Therapy (1969)*, Wolpe classified assertive behaviour into two types of assertive expression:

1. Affectionate expression – expressing affections in appropriate ways

2. Oppositional expression – expressing opposition or making demands of others in socially appropriate ways

Wolpe's view was that people who lack assertiveness experience anxiety or fear, which causes them to worry about:

(a) Embarrassing themselves by expressing affection and being rejected or criticized for it

(a) Upsetting others and being criticized or hurting others.

Wolpe suggested that therapists can help people to deal with both of these problems by encouraging 'patients' to express themselves in assertive ways in a situation where they are likely to meet with success rather than rejection or failure. The therapist then reinforces that success by praising the patient for the assertive expression and encouraging further similar efforts in situations likely to produce success.

Two useful points to remember from the work of Wolpe are:

- While assertiveness often produces very good results for you, it is not necessarily appropriate for *every* situation

- You may find it helpful to practise assertiveness *first* in situations where your prospects of success are good, or the downsides of not succeeding are not too severe. For example, you might consider practising your assertiveness techniques on a door-to-door salesman trying to sell you a product before you move on to practising assertive behaviour in important personal relationships. The idea is that you will then have greater confidence and greater assertiveness skills by the time you start to try out your assertiveness techniques in more difficult situations, or in relationships that are more important to you.

Robert Alberti and Michael Emmons

Rights and equality in relationships

In 1970, the first edition of Robert Alberti and Michael Emmons' book *Your Perfect Right: Assertiveness and Equality In Your Life and Relationships* was published. As the title implied, this book highlighted that becoming assertive involves an awareness of and belief in your rights. In particular, the authors encouraged people to express themselves assertively as a means of improving the quality of and equality in their relationships.

Two key features of the views of Alberti and Emmons which are now accepted by many commentators on assertiveness and which underpin the suggestions in this book are:

- Assertiveness involves standing up for yourself and your rights in a reasonable way

- Assertiveness involves expressing yourself in a way that is respectful of others.

Alberti and Emmons' approach implicitly viewed assertiveness as involving a set of skills that can be learned. In line with this view, they encouraged the use of some sensible measures to help you build those skills, including:

- Set yourself practical goals for what you want to achieve in relation to your assertiveness and order them in priority

- Keep a daily record of issues and your progress in relation to them in an assertiveness journal. Alberti and Emmons recommend covering five aspects in your journal:

    (i) Situations (i.e. specific times and occasions where you might have the opportunity or be challenged to act assertively)

(ii) People (who might impact one way or another on your success in acting assertively)

(iii) Attitudes, thoughts and beliefs (i.e. your own views and thoughts that may be impacting on how you act and whether you behave assertively)

(iv) Behaviours (a record of how you actually do act)

(v) Obstacles that seem to make it harder for you to act assertively (these might include mental or emotional blocks, difficulties or a lack of assertiveness skills in a particular situation).

Manuel J. Smith

In 1974 Manuel J Smith wrote the bestselling book *When I Say No, I Feel Guilty* which provided a well developed programme for addressing assertiveness issues.

Rights and responsibilities

Smith's book was built around ten 'assertive rights' which he saw as providing the basis for healthy participation in relationships. He highlighted a primary right from which he said all other assertive rights are derived: the right to be your own judge of everything that you are and do. In line with this primary right, he saw assertiveness as being as much about *taking responsibility* for your own actions, thoughts and behaviour as about having rights which you can exercise. Rights in Smith's view involve having the courage to make your own choices and decisions, as well as the courage to admit when you make mistakes.

Evolution and assertiveness

Smith set his analysis of assertiveness in the context of evolutionary responses to anxiety. He saw 'fight' or 'flight' as primitive responses triggered by anxiety in the face of danger. He argued that, in modern society, verbal problem-solving provides a new dimension for human beings to use in the face of anxiety, in place of these primitive responses of fight or flight which served our forebears well but which aren't always suited to our complex modern environment and social interchanges.

In his book, Smith described and explained a number of specific verbal techniques to use in communicating with and responding to other people in an assertive way. These have become classic techniques for developing assertive communication skills, and some of them have been covered in this book, including the broken record technique, fogging, negative assertion and negative inquiry (see chapter 3).

Smith recognized that some of his suggested techniques work better in particular types of relationship. He distinguished between three basic types of relationship:

1. Commercial or formal relationships, such as when you are in a shop buying a product

2. Authority relationships, such as your relationship with your boss

3. Equality relationships, i.e. relationships between equals such as friends or neighbours

Smith's recognition that your assertiveness may vary depending on the different types of relationship you are in is useful. To his three categories we might add a fourth category, that of *intimate relationships* – particularly your relationship with your partner, if you have one. Smith himself devoted a separate chapter to very close relationships, although he didn't treat it as a separate category in his initial analysis of basic types of relationship. When you try out the suggestions in this book for building your assertiveness, you may find it helpful to reflect on which category or categories of relationship you find it most difficult to act assertively in, and which techniques you find most helpful for those particular categories of relationship.

Assertiveness for women

Assertiveness training really started to become fashionable in the 1970s and 80s when it was enthusiastically taken up by the women's liberation movement. In those two decades, assertiveness training often featured as a core component in self-development groups and classes for women in North America, the UK and Europe, as a way of helping women to stand up for their rights both in individual relationships and in a wider political context. There are many assertiveness books and guides specifically aimed at women and intended to help women with particular issues arising from:

- Socialization of women – expectations of girls and women to fulfil certain social or gender based roles, to avoid expressing personal views or wishes assertively, or to put the needs of others first

- Political, professional or societal structures leading to discrimination against women and difficulties for women in achieving personal or professional goals

- Marginalizing or lack of awareness of women's needs and desires within particular groups or environments, so that a conscious effort is needed to bring attention to relevant issues and to address them proactively.

There is a range of approaches in the literature and views about women and assertiveness issues. This is not a static topic because attitudes in society can change and norms within different cultures vary. One of the most popular books from the 1970s when assertiveness training for women first became prominent is considered below.

The Assertive Woman – Stanlee Phelps and Nancy Austin

In their book, *The Assertive Woman* (first published in 1975, updated with new material in 1997), Stanlee Phelps and Nancy Austin explored assertiveness from a number of different angles and made constructive suggestions as to how to increase your assertiveness. They focused in particular on issues that might be relevant for women but they also included ideas which men struggling with assertiveness issues might be able to make use of.

Developing assertiveness characteristics
A useful aspect of the approach adopted by Phelps and Austin was that they illustrated how particular personality types may be embodied in particular women in particular situations. *The Assertive Woman* included hypothetical characters to illustrate four different personality types: passive, aggressive, indirect and assertive. (This book builds on a similar classification although it tends to focus more on situations than on personality types). The authors gave these four characters the names Dorrie Doormat, Augusta Aggressive, Isabel Indirect and Alison Assertive. They also offered some male counterparts: Dan Doormat, Arnold Aggressive, Iago Indirect and Alex Assertive. Phelps and Austin provided a complex analysis of the features of these character types. Throughout their book they indicated the different ways in which each character type might act or react in a particular situation, while acknowledging that most people are a mixture of all four types. You may find that you can identify friends or people you know who have strong tendencies towards one or other of the four types of character described.

Labels and myths about women
Phelps and Austin observed in their book a number of different ways in which women might label themselves

or see themselves (sometimes unconsciously) as having to act in certain ways. For example, they referred to the *compassion trap* highlighted by Margaret Adams – believing as a woman that you exist in order to serve others and that you should always show compassion and tenderness to others. They also highlighted a number of myths that people might believe about women which could make it difficult for women to progress or be heard. For example, in a working environment women may be labelled as over-emotional or insecure or expected to work extra hard to prove themselves.

Phelps and Austin provided a range of useful practical suggestions for dealing with these labels from others or from yourself, many of which are consistent with the ideas in this book. An additional feature of their work which comes through strongly is the idea that slowing down, meditating and practising deep muscle relaxation can help you to get in tune with yourself and detach yourself from those mental and psychological pressures to act or be a certain way.

They also encouraged readers to use positive visualization exercises to help imagine acting, thinking and feeling assertively, as well as suggesting that you create and remind yourself of affirmations about your own potential and abilities, in order to help reinforce positive self-image and belief in your ability to become assertive and develop your own identity (see p. 112 for suggestions as to a positive visualization exercise that you can use to help you act more assertively).

Rational Emotive Behaviour Therapy (REBT) – Albert Ellis

As already highlighted, some of the early theorists in the field of assertiveness such as Salter and Wolpe focused in particular on practising assertive *behaviour* as a way of developing your assertiveness. In the second half of the twentieth century different approaches were developed towards assertiveness and other self-development issues, which began to tackle assertiveness issues at the level of *thinking*, at least as much as at the level of action, and those ideas have formed a major influence on the suggestions in my book. One of the principal pioneers in approaching self-development in this way was the psychologist Albert Ellis. Ellis's approach, which he first began to use in the mid 1950s and developed over subsequent decades, enabled people to change self-defeating thought patterns by helping them to see the irrationality, inflexibility or self defeating nature of some of their beliefs. Ellis initially called his approach *rational therapy* and it was later renamed *rational emotive therapy* or *rational emotive behaviour therapy*.

The umbrella term *cognitive behavioural therapy* ('CBT') is also sometimes used to describe approaches such as Ellis's, which incorporate techniques for dealing with thinking patterns, related emotions and behaviour in a clear model or system. In his work Ellis showed that the beliefs we have about the significance of situations or ourselves or about events or actions of others are important in influencing how we feel and how we act. His approach was influenced by the thinking of ancient Greek philosophers such as Epictetus who held that:

> 'Men are disturbed not by things, but by the view which they take of them.'

The ABC model of emotions

Ellis developed a model for looking at the relation between your thought patterns and your emotions, which is often used in assertiveness training as well as to help in dealing with other emotional or behavioural issues. In its initial formulation this model was called the ABC model of emotions. It has come to be one of the most widely-used methods in cognitive behavioural therapy ('CBT'). The model analysed the development of emotions in the following sequence:

(A): Activating Event → **(B)** Belief → **(C)** Consequences (Emotional and behavioural).

Ellis's ABC model and his suggestions for challenging or questioning distorted thinking processes have many possible applications. Chapters 4 and 5 of this book include explanations of how his ideas can be used to help change or deal with the thought processes involved in passive or aggressive behaviour in an effective way. The practical approach that he advocated is endorsed in the overall framework of this book, which has aimed to show how rational and analytical techniques can be used to help you develop your assertiveness and enable you to benefit accordingly from a fruitful life and relationships.

Appendix 2 – Assessing your assertiveness

Here are some possible answers to the questions given in the introduction (p. 12). For each question four sample responses are given that might be considered (a) passive, (b) directly aggressive, (c) indirectly aggressive and (d) assertive. To some degree this is a subjective judgement, but the suggested responses give an indication of the kinds of reaction that might be considered as falling within each style of response. Compare your own likely reactions with the suggested alternatives to get an idea of whether you have a general tendency to use one of the four styles of response more than others, or whether your style of response is quite varied and depends on the type of situation or people involved.

1. At work, a project comes up that you are very interested in working on. Your team leader asks everyone in the team if they would like to be involved. You and two others say 'yes' when asked. What do you then do, given that you want to be involved but so do others?

(a) Defer to the others and say that you'll be happy for them to take it on, as they will probably be better at it than you.

(b) Highlight several (alleged) weaknesses in the others' work and say that they aren't the right people for the task.

(c) Say that you're happy to go with whatever everyone wants but then later, after the work has been given to one of the other two, highlight that person's (alleged) weaknesses to one of your other colleagues and you say what a bad decision it was to give the work to that person.

(d) Explain clearly the level of your interest and explore with the others whether there is a constructive way of you all working on the project, or, if it is not possible for you all to work on it, then agree what would be the fairest way of deciding who gets to work on it.

2. You and your partner are out a restaurant having a meal with friends. During the meal, your partner keeps making dismissive remarks towards you. How do you react?

(a) Not say anything about it then or later.

(b) Scowl at your partner and tell him/her to **** off.

(c) Act as if nothing has happened but badmouth him/her to all your friends later.

(d) Ask him/her if you've done something to upset him/her and explain that you find his/her remarks dismissive.

3. You receive an unsolicited telephone call from a caller offering a service to install solar glazing panels on your roof, which you have no interest in. How do you respond?

(a) Listen to five minutes of marketing information.

(b) Swear at the caller and slam the phone down.

(c) Go along politely with what the caller is saying without committing to anything, then talk about them in disparaging terms to your partner as soon as the phone call ends.

(d) Politely intervene as soon as you realize what the call is about, say that you are not interested in the service and end the call.

4. You are watching your favourite television programme when your flatmate comes in, takes the remote control, asks if you mind watching another programme and switches channel before you have a chance to object. How do you react?

(a) Not say anything and watch their programme with them.

(b) Grab the remote control back, shout at them and switch channels back.

(c) Go along with them without saying anything, but devise a series of ways of getting back at them.

(d) Explain that you were watching the programme and offer to record their programme for them.

5. You have just bought a new sweater which you rather like. When you meet up with your friend in a café the next day she notices it straightaway and remarks: 'Ouch, that colour doesn't suit you at all.' What do you reply?

(a) Say, 'I suppose it is rather bright.'

(b) Make a disparaging remark about something she is wearing.

(c) Smile and laugh about it in an accepting way, then 'accidentally' spill some coffee on her blouse a few minutes later.

(d) Say, 'I like it – I think it goes quite well with these trousers. What is it you think it doesn't match with?'

For each of the above questions:

Answer (a) is a sample **passive** response.
Answer (b) is a sample **directly aggressive** response.
Answer (c) is a sample **indirectly aggressive** response.
Answer (d) is a sample **assertive** response.

Additional resources

The books listed below (in alphabetical order) provide useful information and ideas for improving your assertiveness.

Assertiveness Step by Step by Dr Windy Dryden and Daniel Constantinou (Sheldon Press, 2004)

A Woman in Your Own Right: Assertiveness and You by Anne Dickson (Quartet Books, 1982)

How to Keep People From Pushing Your Buttons by Dr Albert Ellis and Dr Arthur Lange (Citadel Press, 1994)

Overcoming Anxiety: A self-help guide using Cognitive Behavioral Techniques by Helen Kennerley (Robinson Publishing Ltd, 1997)

The Assertive Woman by Stanlee Phelps and Nancy Austin (Impact Publishers, 2002)

The Practice of Behavior Therapy by Joseph Wolpe (Pergamon General Psychology Series 1, 1992)

When I Say No, I Feel Guilty: How to Cope – Using the Skills of Systematic Assertive Therapy by Manuel J. Smith, PhD (Mass Market Paperback, 1975)

Your Perfect Right: Assertiveness and Equality in Your Life and Relationships by Robert Alberti, PhD and Michael Emmons, PhD (Impact Publishers, 2008)

Website resources

Downloadable self-help guides to being assertive can be found at: http://www.moodjuice.scot.nhs.uk/assertiveness. asp and http://www.heron.nhs.uk/pidd/publicationdetails. aspx?formatid=12392

Author's website

Information about life coaching and ebooks on a variety of self-help topics such as assertiveness, self-esteem, anxiety, life change and cognitive behavioural therapy techniques can be found at David Bonham-Carter's life coaching website: www.davidbonham-carter.com

Index